STREET BY STREET

HISTORIC
ALEXANDRIA
VIRGINIA
STREET BY STREET

A SURVEY OF
EXISTING
EARLY BUILDINGS

BY ETHELYN COX

HISTORIC
ALEXANDRIA
FOUNDATION

DISTRIBUTED BY
EPM PUBLICATIONS
McLEAN, VIRGINIA

EDITING: *Jean E. Keith*
DESIGN: *Howard E. Paine*
PRODUCTION: *Peggy Simsarian*
PHOTOGRAPHY: *Russell Jones*
   Victor Amato, Nina Leake
PUBLICATIONS COMMITTEE:
John Howard Joynt, Chairman
Ethelyn Cox
Jean E. Keith
Mangum Weeks

ACKNOWLEDGMENTS

We thank Worth Bailey, who compiled the inventory of surviving early buildings; William J. Murtagh, Keeper of the National Register of Historic Places, and President of the Victorian Society, who wrote the Foreword. Margaret D. Calhoun, Gertrude Frankel, Jeanne Plitt and Marjorie Tallichet, of the Alexandria Library, who supplied essential material; Alvin W. Frinks, Clerk of the Circuit Court of the City of Alexandria, his staff, and Donald C. Wells, who provided guidance in using court records; Edith Moore Sprouse, who shared her extensive notes on items in early Alexandria newspapers; Alexandra Carlisle, who searched for and summarized comments of early travelers who visited Alexandria; Frances Maigne, who assisted in scanning early newspapers and provided material from the National Archives; John Heatwole, who prepared digests of the papers of Charles Simms and other material relating to Alexandria in the Library of Congress; Jean Elliot, who made available her research on early Alexandria families and churches; Patrick Butler, who provided a paraphrase of a letter of Benjamin H. Latrobe regarding the building at 209, 211 North Fairfax; Margery Hall Fawcett, for information on St. Paul's Church; Mr. and Mrs. Franklin L. Thatcher, who prepared digests of deeds in Fairfax Court House that relate to Alexandria properties; the Alexandria Tourist Council, who supplied the photographs of Lyceum Hall and the 100 block of Prince; and most of all, Alexandria's historians, whose writings have furnished information about Alexandria's early buildings and the people who built them and lived in them. Finally, we are indebted to the late Maria E. K. Van Swearingen, who located many of Alexandria's early records in the Virginia State Library.

FOREWORD

Alexandria, despite its early boosters, was never destined to be a great commercial and industrial center. It was not created by successive explosive growths, characteristic of so many American cities, which destroyed the evidences of earlier building. Instead, Alexandria formed more gradually as a collection of residences of architectural quality with sufficient commercial entities to serve those residences.

The Congressional action of March 1791, which included Alexandria in the new District of Columbia, prohibited the construction of public buildings on the Virginia side of the river and thus strengthened the residential character of Alexandria. The announced intention of siting the new capital across the river caused the first noticeable building boom in the last decade of the 18th century. Curiously enough, the second such surge came within a few years after the retrocession of the Virginia portion of the District of Columbia to that state in 1846. Just prior to the Civil War, within a period of some forty-eight months, the city added over seven hundred buildings to its inventory.

Conservative taste in Alexandria carried 18th century stylistic details into the 19th century. The tendency, therefore, has been to think of the older part of the city as being solely 18th century. This concept, of course, obscures the rich continuum of daily life over many decades of the 18th and 19th centuries which the buildings actually reflect. This misconception was heavily reinforced by the presence of George Washington as a prominent 18th century figure in the town and by the continued existence of a number of landmark buildings such as Gadsby's Tavern and Christ Church with which he is irrevocably intertwined.

As a result, such landmark buildings as these, and those associated with Robert E. Lee and other prominent Alexandrians, serve as pivotal points in an area that has a highly developed sense of identity and place. However, without the many supporting buildings of age which line the streets of the city, such landmarks would stand as isolated and forlorn entities, unrelated to their environment.

As Alexandria enters its third century, it retains to a remarkable extent the continuity of its early streetscapes. It has largely survived the onslaughts of the throw-away mentality of our 20th century society. If anything, there appears to be a growing sensitivity to the overall values that intensify the quality of "place" in the city. Restoration and rehabilitation continue. But there is also a new awareness of the importance of the amenities of the urban streetscape. The city is planting trees, laying brick sidewalks, burying utility lines, and increasing its control over advertising graphics.

Although this book stresses historical associations, one cannot, after all, see history. What one does see, unfolding from the river to the railroad, is a reflection of time and growth. Collectively, these individual units range from local to national in historical significance and from vernacular to sophisticated in architectural design. As a total conservation neighborhood, the Historic District has few peers in the country, and certainly none in the greater Washington area. The local government sensed this in 1946 when it passed the local zoning ordinance defining the Old and Historic Alexandria District, restricting the changes permitted by private property owners to what was then considered to be an inordinate degree. That this was one of the first such local actions in our country is noteworthy.

Higher government authorities subsequently confirmed the importance of preserving this neighborhood. The Department of the Interior in 1966 applied National Landmark status to the port area. In 1969, upon application by the Commonwealth of Virginia, the Department of the Interior included the entire district on the National Register of Historic Places.

Unlike Williamsburg and Sturbridge Village, Alexandria is not an outdoor museum. It continues as a living urban community with some museum elements. The preservability of this conservation area and its ultimate limits cannot be dictated by arbitrary protective dates or boundary lines. The 100-year sliding scale recently adopted for the protection of buildings in the district was a recognition of the worth of structures beyond the former cut-off year of 1846, since many buildings beyond that date were already being renovated at a rapid rate. As for the boundaries, physical features such as the Potomac River and a railroad line would appear to be the ultimate natural determinants.

To quote from the publication *With Heritage So Rich*, "if we wish to have a future with greater meaning, we must concern ourselves not only with the historic highlights, but we must be concerned with the total heritage . . . all that is worth preserving from the past as a living part of the present." Further, to be successful, "intensive thought and study must be given to economic conditions and tax policies which will affect our efforts to preserve such areas as living parts of the community."

INTRODUCTION

This book is one of several projects sponsored by the Historic Alexandria Foundation to encourage interest in the renovation and restoration of early buildings in Alexandria. It includes buildings of architectural and historical significance. It also includes buildings that, standing alone, would be of minor importance, but standing together, preserve early street facades that evoke Alexandria's early history.

In 1959 the Foundation commissioned Worth Bailey, an Architectural Historian with the Historic American Buildings Survey, National Park Service, Department of the Interior, to list surviving early buildings in the Old Town area. The survey covered buildings that from their exterior architectural features might date from the mid-late 18th century through (and in a few cases beyond) the mid 19th century. Mr. Bailey completed the survey in 1962. A year later the Planning Department of the City of Alexandria published the list-ings, with appropriate sectional maps.

Russell Jones and Victor Amato photographed the buildings during the years 1959–1962 and 1964–1968, respectively. Nina Leake has supplied additional photographs 1973–1975.

The Foundation designed a plaque and made it available, for a fee, to owners of the buildings. The plaque is keyed to a map and provides a registry number for each building. The registry number is composed of three parts: first, the number assigned to the square block in which the building is located; second, a letter identifying the north, south, east or west face of that block; and third, the street number of the building.

Late in 1968 the author began to assemble material to be used in this book. It was decided that it would not be possible to research or include photographs of all buildings listed. Decisions as to which buildings to include were difficult. Some basically good buildings disfigured by uninspired alterations were selected to encourage restoration. A few buildings in areas where little restoration has occurred were included—again to encourage restoration.

In 1974 the 1959–1962 inventory was reviewed. Buildings that had been demolished were deleted, and renovations and restorations noted. The revised inventory lists 897 buildings. Of these, 576 buildings are included in the 374 photographs used. The 321 buildings that are not illustrated are listed with their inventory descriptions. As we go to press, this book gives the Foundation's current inventory of surviving early buildings in downtown Alexandria.

Using early deed and will books, the author developed a partial chain of title for each building researched. The original town lots, except for the waterfront lots and the marsh lots on the first northern boundary of the town, were each one half an acre, or a quarter of a city block. These original town lots were subdivided as the town grew. It is assumed that, with a few exceptions, any existing building dates, at the earliest, from the time of the subdivision. In the many cases when an early building on a lot has been replaced, determination as to the approximate date of the existing building has been based on its architectural style. The author also assumed that a substantial increase in the sale price indicated that a property had been improved, either by the addition of a building, or by the renovation and enlargement of an existing building. Early sources, such as insurance policies, tax records, and newspaper notices and advertisements, frequently supplied useful information. Many determinations remain qualified and tentative. The Foundation hopes that this book will stimulate further research on Alexandria's early buildings, as new information becomes available.

1730–1748 Nothing remains of the early settlement that grew up around the 1730 tobacco warehouse at the foot of Oronoco Street. The site was in Prince William County until 1742, when the county was divided and the northern part became Fairfax County. The topographical map drawn by George Washington, showing Hugh West's house and warehouse, and noting the advantages of the terrain, was probably prepared in 1748 to assist those, led by Washington's half-brother Lawrence, who petitioned the Virginia Assembly to establish a new town.

1749–1762 The petitioners succeeded. The Virginia Assembly established the town of Alexandria by an act approved May 11, 1749. Traditionally, George Washington assisted in surveying the town. The official map, prepared by John West, Jr., Deputy Surveyor of Fairfax County, shows the town divided into 84 lots that were offered for sale July 13–14, 1749. No one could buy more than two lots. Each purchaser was required, within two years after conveyance, to build on his lot a house of brick, stone or wood, at least twenty feet square and nine feet high, with a brick or stone chimney. If the purchaser owned two adjoining lots, he could build one house "proportionally (sic) thereto." West's map shows two lots, or half a block, set aside for a market place. In April 1752 Governor Dinwiddie issued a proclamation moving the Fairfax County Court to Alexandria, and a court house was built on the market place.

The act of 1749 named eleven trustees, who were authorized to "establish such rules and orders for the more regular placing of the houses . . . as to them shall seem meet." In July 1752 the trustees approved a resolution requiring "all dwelling houses not begun or to be built hereafter . . . to be in line with the street as chief of the houses now are, and that no gable or end of such house be on or next to the street." Thus, within a few years of the founding of the town, the trustees laid down the primary regulations which resulted in solid rows of town houses built along the street line. The imposing stone mansion of John Carlyle and the simple frame structure of the Ramsay House were built or begun before the restrictive resolution was adopted. Both are situated within the same block as though to instruct us in contrasting architectural styles.

In March 1755 a Mrs. Browne arrived in Alexandria with Braddock's troops. She found Alexandria "as agreeable a place as could be expected, it being inhabited but 4 years." She was obliged "to take a room but little larger than to hold my bed, and not so much as a chair in it."

Around 1760 a traveler described the town as "a small trading place," situated on an arc of a "large circular bay . . . at one extremity of which is a wharf; at the other a dock for building ships."

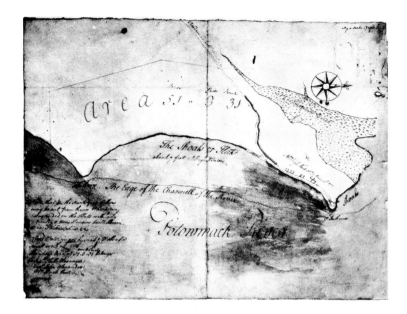

1748 *Topographical map of the original site of Alexandria, probably prepared by George Washington for the use of his half-brother Lawrence in persuading the Virginia Assembly to establish the town. (Library of Congress.)*

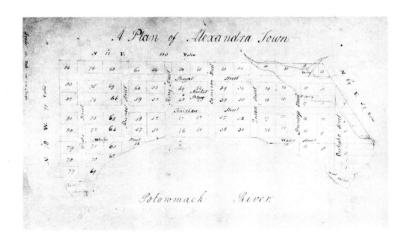

1749 *Map of John West, Jr., Deputy Surveyor of Fairfax County, showing the first town boundaries and lots. (Alexandria Deed Book H, Alexandria Hustings Court, p. 332.)*

1763 *Map of George West, Surveyor of Fairfax County, showing in broken lines the lots the Virginia Assembly added to the town in November 1762. (Library of Congress.)*

1763–1798 The March 10, 1763, map of George West, Surveyor of Fairfax County, shows in broken lines the lots added to the town by a November 1762 act of the Virginia Assembly. The town trustees sold the new lots on May 9, 1763. This was the second and last such sale by the trustees. Washington bought two lots. Three years later he became a town trustee.

Washington also represented Fairfax County in the House of Burgesses in 1765, although he was not present when Patrick Henry offered his resolutions on the Stamp Act. This act, opposed by the most powerful and articulate of the colonists, was repealed. But Parliament passed new revenue acts, also resented by the colonists. Locally this opposition was expressed in the Fairfax Resolves, drafted by George Mason of Gunston Hall, and adopted July 18, 1774, at a

meeting in the court house in Alexandria, with Washington presiding.

In 1774 John Alexander laid off and sold lots adjoining the town. His conveyances continued the requirement that the lots be built upon within two years. In October 1779, because of "the scarcity and difficulty of procuring building materials" during the Revolution, the Virginia Assembly extended the time for building to within two years after the end of hostilities. A young Englishman who arrived in Alexandria in 1775 noted "several good brick buildings." A traveler passing through in May 1777 found the houses "mostly wooden and small," but described the brick Episcopal and Presbyterian churches as "large and neat."

During the Revolution the town served as an assembly and distribution center for troops and supplies. A fort was built upon Jones Point. In July 1776 and the spring of 1781 enemy vessels approached but did no damage to the town.

In October 1779 the Virginia Assembly made Alexandria a port of entry. During the same session Alexandria was incorporated, and its freeholders authorized to elect annually "twelve fit and able men," the twelve to elect "from their own body," a mayor, recorder and four aldermen, the remaining six to serve as common councilmen. The first mayor of Alexandria, elected in February 1780, was Robert Townshend Hooe.

After the war ended, construction began, encouraged by the influx of those who thought Alexandria a good place to be as the new nation faced its uncertain but hopeful future. Owners of lands adjoining the town divided them into lots and sold them. As these lots were improved, the Virginia

Assembly, at various times, extended the boundaries of the town to include them.

A visitor in 1785 observed: "Alexandria had made considerable advances since '78, but afforded no comparison, in its progress, to its vigorous rival, Baltimore."

In April 1789, Alexandrians, predominantly Federalists, celebrated the ratification of the Constitution with a dinner, which Washington attended.

Congress, meeting in New York City in July 1790, approved the transfer of the federal capital to Philadelphia for ten years, pending removal to the new city of Washington to be built along the Potomac River on land ceded by Virginia and Maryland. In March 1791, Congress, in session in Philadelphia, amended the 1790 act to permit the town of Alexandria, and a part of Fairfax County (to be called Alexandria County) to be included in the District of Columbia. The act prohibited the construction of any public buildings on the Virginia side of the river.

Around 1790, a young merchant from London noted that the town was then mainly one street, running northeast and southwest. This was Fairfax Street. Wooden houses predominated—"a few good ones of brick," but "no remarkable buildings worthy of a stranger's attention." Another traveler found the town smaller than Baltimore, and "quite as irregular in its construction and quite as muddy." He conceded that there was more lux-ury in Alexandria, "if a miserable luxury: you see servants in silk stockings, and their masters in boots." He also noted "superb wharves" and "vast warehouses," although "the expected commerce languishes." Paving of the streets began in the early 1790's. The stone "best calculated for paving is of an oval kind, weighing from fifteen pounds to sixty pounds." The source was usually "the River Potomac near the Little Falls."

The future seemed bright. In November 1792 the Virginia Assembly chartered the Bank of Alexandria, the first to be established in Virginia. In 1795 a visitor was impressed by the "vast number" of buildings under construction. A year later, one traveler found Alexandria "beyond all comparison the handsomest town in Virginia," and another visitor proclaimed it "one of the neatest towns in the United States, the houses being mostly of brick." A good example of this handsome late 18th century construction which impressed these visitors can be found in "Gentry Row," the 200 block of Prince Street.

The 1790's were difficult years for Alexandria and other seaports. The French were seizing American vessels in retaliation for the concessions made by the United States to Great Britain in the Jay Treaty. One source estimates that at least twenty Alexandria vessels were captured. By 1798 Alexandrians were preparing for war with their former ally. Beginning in April, and extending into the spring of

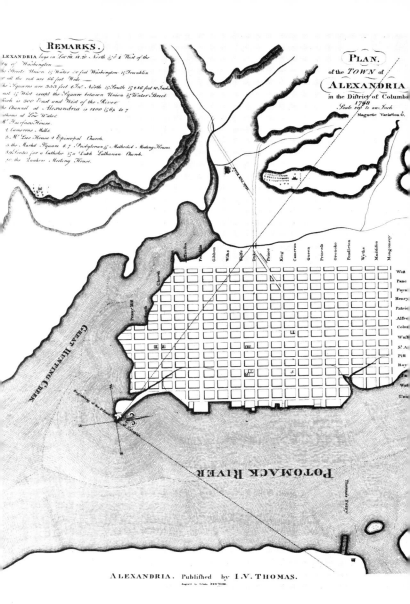

1799 Map of George Gilpin, local surveyor, showing the town boundaries as enlarged by acts of the Virginia Assembly 1785–1798. (Library of Congress.)

References

A. Market House ~ Court House
B. Church
C. Roman Church
D. German Lutheran Church
E. Quakers Meeting House
F. Presbyterian
G. Methodist
H. The new Theatre
I. Academy

Mr. Fairfax's House

1799, town meetings were held "to consider the critical situation of the country," and local military companies met and drilled.

1799–1844 By 1798 the Virginia Assembly had extended Alexandria's boundaries to include the streets shown on the map of George Gilpin, issued in 1799, the year that Washington died. An unofficial map recorded in an 1803 Alexandria deed book shows the boundaries of the District of Columbia as they related to Alexandria. A comparison of the 1799 and 1803 maps with the 1749 map shows the land added by fill along the riverfront during the town's first fifty years.

In February 1801 Congress provided a circuit court and various court officials for the District, but for the most part the laws of Virginia would remain in effect in the territory ceded by Virginia until Congress provided otherwise.

In 1802 a local newspaper noted a revival in trade: "Not more than two years since it was a rare thing to see a square rigged vessel in our harbour; we now have our wharfs lined with vessels destined for distant ports." The revival of trade was short-lived. A yellow fever epidemic in 1803 closed the port for several months. A tabulation of death notices between August 20 and October 25 shows that at least 156 persons died. Many fled the town.

A year later a visitor found the town "mostly of brick," many buildings being a "good stile (sic) of architecture." Buildings going up west of Washington Street at this time included 817, 819 Prince (1803), 915, 917 King (1802), and 1101–1111 Prince (1804–1806).

According to a traveler in 1808, the Embargo Act of 1807 prohibiting trade abroad "very much checked the enterprising and commercial spirit" that had prevailed in Alexandria. However, he found

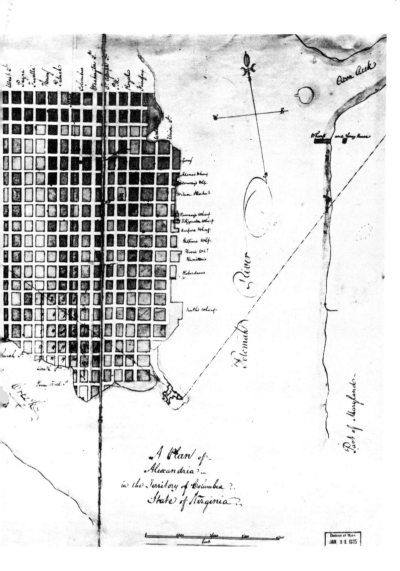

the streets "well paved, of an extensive width, and kept perfectly clean." He admired the brick buildings, "some of them very stately and elegant." That autumn another visitor noted "little appearance of improvement since my last visit, three years ago." He was told that the town then had around 6,000 inhabitants and 1,780 buildings.

The Embargo Act was repealed in 1809. The town enjoyed a brief period of prosperity, shipping grain

1803 Map of unknown surveyor showing boundaries of Alexandria as a part of the District of Columbia. (Alexandria Deed Book G, Circuit Court of the District of Columbia for the County of Alexandria, p. 465.)

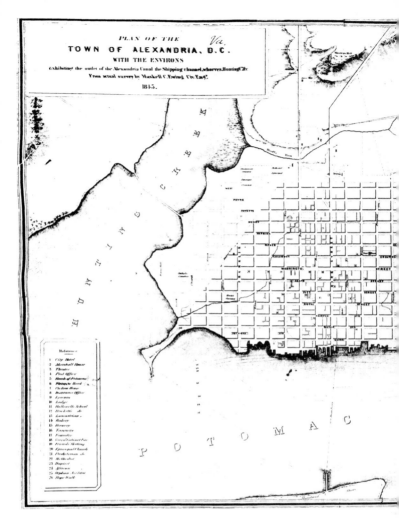

1845 *Map of Maskell C. Ewing showing Alexandria before retrocession to Virginia in 1846. (Library of Congress.)*

abroad to feed a Europe at war. Building resumed around 1810–1818. The Bank of Alexandria was joined by other banks between 1804 and 1817.

Some of Alexandria's young men served in the War of 1812. The town was not disturbed until late in August 1814, when the British, after burning Washington City, sent their fleet to Alexandria. Alexandria, undefended because the local militia had been sent to the defense of the capital, surrendered. The British seized the ships in port and loaded them with the tobacco,

flour, cotton, wine and sugar they found in Alexandria's warehouses.

A survey of Alexandria buildings, recorded in the Council minutes in the spring of 1817, lists 512 brick and 383 frame three-story and two-story houses and warehouses; 429 one and one-half story buildings (380 dwelling houses and 49˙ warehouses); seven places of worship; the academy building, and two Lancasterian Schools. There were also 51 sheds occupied by blacksmiths, tanners, boatbuilders, wheelwrights, joiners, cabinet makers, and other work-men. The national financial crisis in 1819 was reflected in Alexandria by numerous newspaper notices of sales of Alexandria properties by the United States Marshal, and by the editorial comment: "Our country has for the last twelve months felt the frowns of Hard Times."

In the early 1800's obituaries of Alexandrians who had known Washington and had been prominent in the early years of the town began appearing with increasing frequency. There were also advertisements of those trying to sell local properties prior to moving— to Washington City, or more frequently, to new lands in the west.

The town's entertainment of Lafayette in 1824, and of John Quincy Adams and his cabinet in 1825 were welcome diversions. The Alexandria Canal Company, incorporated in 1830, gave hope for increased trade and commerce. But the Bank of Alexandria failed in 1834, anticipating the national financial panic of 1837.

An 1842 guide to the City of Washington summed it up:

Alexandria received a check in the early part of the century, followed by a long period of vicissitude and depression. But the visitor will be gratified at witnessing many proofs of revived activity, and will observe in the style of recent buildings, sufficient evidence that a new impulse has been communicated to the inhabitants.

The "recent buildings" were Lyceum Hall, and two other Greek Revival buildings—the Court House, demolished in the late 19th century, and the Second Presbyterian Church, still standing, but with a restyled facade. Research shows few residential structures built in the 1840's.

1845–1860 The 1845 map lists key numbers for twenty-six places of interest, and shows the outlet of the Alexandria Canal, which had disappointed expectations. In 1846 the Virginia Assembly agreed to accept the retrocession of Alexandria and Alexandria County, and Congress agreed to hold a referendum. On September 1 and 2, residents of the town and county, by a vote of 763 to 222, approved retrocession. A year later the Virginia Assembly chartered the first railroad to serve Alexandria. Numerous railroad charters followed, some acquired later by the Southern Railway system.

In December 1850 there were 1,359 dwelling houses, and 92 "manufactories" in Alexandria, and the population totalled 8,795. Two years later a visitor commented:

Alexandria may be said to be a *finished* city. It bears upon it all the marks of decay . . . There were many comfortable residences, but the crumbling wall, the neglected hut, the deserted streets and propped up tenement, spoke eloquently of the absence of enterprise and capital.

As these melancholy observations were being made, the Virginia Assembly was considering the act that in May 1852 made Alexandria a city. Perhaps the greatest construction period in Alexandria's early history followed. In April 1854 the *Alexandria Gazette* announced: "Seven hundred houses have been built in the City during the last three years." Many of the buildings constructed in this building boom were commodious three-story Greek Revival town dwellings of pressed brick with ornate molded brick cornices. Good examples may be seen in the 400 and 500 blocks of Duke, Prince, and Cameron, and in the 300 block of South St. Asaph. During the early 1850's a gas works was built at the foot of Oronoco Street, and the Alexandria Water Company began operations. Building slowed in 1855, although twenty-two structures were erected between March and August, and some existing buildings were repaired and remodeled.

All local enterprise halted when Union troops occupied Alexandria in 1861. During the war years, public buildings and large dwelling houses were used as hospitals, jails, and as offices and residences for the occupying military and civil establishments.

Postscript The survival of many early buildings may be attributed, in part, to the adversities that kept Alexandria from developing into a major industrial center. Restoration and renovation began around 1930, and accelerated during the years of World War II, when the increase in the Federal government extended the search for lodgings into nearby Virginia and Maryland. Restoration has continued in the downtown residential area, and has spread to the early commercial district. Interest has also developed in the preservation of Victorian buildings of the late 19th century. Demolition protection within the Old and Historic Alexandria District, formerly accorded to buildings constructed in or prior to 1846, has recently been granted to all buildings as they become one hundred years old. The Historic Alexandria Foundation sponsored this change, enlisting the support of national and state preservation groups, and the following local organizations:

The Alexandria Association
The Alexandria Historical
    Restoration and Preservation
    Commission
The Alexandria Historical
    Society
The Alexandria Tourist Council
The Old Town Civic
    Association

The streets are arranged alphabetically in the text, beginning with Alfred and ending with Wolfe.

Buildings on streets running east and west are numbered westward beginning at the river.

Buildings on streets running north and south are numbered in each direction from King Street.

Buildings are arranged in the sequence the visitor sees them as he walks from North to South or from East to West.

224, 226. Probably built by Joseph Birch, to whom Charles Alexander conveyed the lot in 1812. Thirteen years later Ezra Lunt became the owner. Lunt's grandfather, for whom he was named, served with Revolutionary troops at Bunker Hill.

Also, **216**, brick, 2 stories, 3 bays wide, shed roof, bracket cornice, mid 19th C.

114. Originally Mechanics' Hall, dedicated by the Mechanic Relief Society of Alexandria in 1818 with Masonic ceremonies. Lyceum Company organized here in November 1838. Purchased by Hugh C. Smith in 1842.

122. May incorporate early buildings on the lot when sold in 1812. By 1822 Edward Smyth was the owner. An inventory of Smyth's estate recorded in 1849 lists "one two-story brick dwelling, one one-and-a-half story frame dwelling, ice house, and stables," on this lot.

107 South. **Friendship Fire Company.** Established 1774. George Washington was a member and donated a fire engine purchased in Philadelphia for £80–10. First engine house on Cameron street side of Market Square. This building dates from 1855. Maintained by the Friendship Veterans Fire Engine Company. Open to the public.

Also South, **111**, clapboard, 2 stories, gable roof, probably mid 19th C., Victorianized; **113**, brick with false front, 2 stories, gable roof, probably early 19th C.; **115**, brick, 3 stories, shed roof, small windows in top floor, modillion cornice, early 19th C.; **117**, brick, 2 stories, gable roof, molded cornice, probably early 19th C.

111. In 1815 Daniel McLean paid $19,500 for a half block on which there were this dwelling house, a sugar refinery, and other buildings and improvements. House probably built 1807–1808 by previous owner, William S. Moore. McLean was chief financial backer of the group that established St. Paul's Church. In 1834 the house was purchased by Hugh C. Smith, son of Hugh Smith.

105. Built by William S. Moore, from whom Hugh Smith purchased it in 1808. Smith came to Alexandria some time before 1796. He prospered as a merchant selling china and glassware. He was living in this house when he died in 1855.

305, 303, 301. At 305, then Duvall's tavern, General Washington was feted by the gentlemen of the town on December 31, 1783; in 1787 Daniel Roberdeau was the occupant; from 1788 to 1791, Charles Lee, then Collector of the Port, was living here; from 1793–1807 it served as the banking house of the Bank of Alexandria. Isaac George bought the house at 303 and the lot of 301 in 1829; he built 301 before 1865.

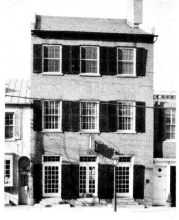

211. Henry Nicholson's dwelling house built around 1805. His biscuit bake house was nearby, on Lee between Cameron and Queen.

311. When advertised for sale in 1817 by owner-builder William Dunlap, a three-story brick with two stories in the rear, running back 117 feet, with 12 rooms, some "spacious and elegant;" with one front, two back stairways; kitchen with two fireplaces; a portico in front; in back a covered way with piazzas; a pantry and smoke house adjoining. "So far" Dunlap had spent over $12,000.

325, 323, 319, 317, 315, 313, 311. Early-mid 19th C. buildings at 325 and 323 replaced early frame houses; those at 319 and 317 are on the site of Cyrus Copper's "Vendue Store." From 1817 until he died in 1830, the oyster house and "refectory" of Dominic Bearcroft, "a respectable colored man," was on the lot of 315. James Campbell built 313 in 1812, and died there, aged 77, in 1821.

Also, **203**, brick, 3 stories, small windows on 3rd floor, early-mid 19 C.

Henry Salkeld was the first owner of the half square fronting on the north side of the 300 block. A Mrs. Browne, who came with Braddock's troops, noted in her diary on May 29, 1755: Received a card from Mrs. Salkeldat (*sic*) . . . [who] desired my Company to her husband's Funeral. . . . He had been dead a Month. It is the Custom of this Place to bury their relations in their Gardens.

CAMERON

South side 300 block, City Hall, completed 1873, south addition 1961. In early days this half square contained the market house; court house; two fire engine houses; town (also school) house; jail, stocks and pillory.

Washington came here when he "went up to Court." Fairfax Court met here 1752–1800; Hustings Court, 1780–1801.

In 1817 a three-story brick market house was built along Royal, steeple designed by "Mr. Latrobe, the architect of the capitol in Washington." The Masonic lodge room and museum of Alexandria Washington Lodge No. 22 was on the third floor. The 1817 building was destroyed by fire in May 1871.

North side 400 block. Thomas Wade West, manager of the Virginia and South Carolina Companies of Comedians, was killed when he fell in the new theater—"inferior to few on the continent, for conveniency, simple elegance and situation"—when it was under construction in 1799. Beside the path leading from Christ Church to its gift shop is his gravestone:

To the Memory of T. W. West
Who Departed This Life
July 28th, 1799
Age 54 Years.

The theater burned in June 1872. Its "charred and blackened walls" may be incorporated, in part, in the buildings at 415–407.

Also, **501,** brick, 3 stories, built by
William Garner 1816; in 1820's residence of Humphrey Peake, Collector
of the Port; in 1831, office of Dr. Orlando Fairfax. **502, 504,** brick, 2½
stories, built by Henry Chatham c.
1812; **506,** brick, 3 stories, early 19th
C.; **512, 514, 516** (512 with false front)
brick, 3 stories, built early-mid 19th C.
by Samuel Bartle, James McNair, and
A. S. Tebbs, respectively.

CAMERON

511. Probably built by James Mc-Veigh around 1850.

509. Contemporary of 507, and also built by William Pomeroy. Thomson F. Mason was the tenant in 1816.

507. In 1804, William Pomeroy who built this house around 1803, conveyed it to Robert Alexander for an annual ground rent of $33.33.

505. Probably built around 1804 by Dr. John Richards.

602. A brick building was on the lot when Anthony Crease, a native of Cornwall, purchased it from heirs of James Parsons in 1811 for $350. In November 1812 the widow of Henry Washington of King George County, Virginia, announced that she had "removed from the Washington Tavern to that new and commodious house lately built by Anthony Crease," and would take in boarders by the day or week. The sale of the house for $2,500 in 1833 suggests that Crease either enlarged or replaced the original building. Now Alexandria Community Y, not affiliated with YWCA.

508. A recent reconstruction on the original lot of Washington's town house, built around 1769, and demolished in 1855. The *Alexandria Gazette* reported on the demolition, noting that the "extreme simplicity of design and almost total absence of ornament" were among the "most impressive features" of the house. The then owner, Benjamin Waters, permitted his friends to take portions of the framework for preservation, "or to be manufactured into cases, and other articles of ornament and use."

CAMERON

606, 608. Samuel Wheeler, whose wife was a daughter of James Parsons, built 606 around 1812.

The house at 608 was new in 1798 when Jean Michael Anthony, Baron Van Havre, bought it from Joseph Thornton. Van Havre was a son-in-law of Henry Joseph, Baron de Stier, who in 1794 brought his family to the United States to escape the French occupation of Belgium. The elder baron built "Riversdale," still standing in Riverdale, Maryland. His daughter Rosalie married George Calvert, brother of Martha Washington's daughter-in-law. House bought in 1803 by Bathurst Daingerfield, a prosperous sea captain. In his will Daingerfield directed that the Orphans' Court of Alexandria was to have nothing to do with his estate, because the court was "loose in their office."

Also, **604**, brick, 3 stories, mid 19th C., replacing "Widow Parson's" early house.

611, 609. In 1795, John Bogue, "joiner and cabinet maker," built 611 for himself, and 609 for James Irwin. General Light Horse Harry Lee brought his family, including three-year-old Robert Edward, from Stratford to 611 in late 1810.

607. Built by William Yeaton, who bought the lot in 1799. Town house of Thomas, ninth Lord Fairfax, from 1830 to 1846; later town house of his son, Dr. Orlando Fairfax. Bryan Fairfax, father of Thomas, was an intimate friend of Washington and an early rector of Christ Church. Thomas' wife was a grand-daughter of John Carlyle.

Also, **909**, clapboard, 2 stories, gable roof, probably early 19th C.; **910**, brick, 3 stories (originally 2½ stories), early 19th C., Victorianized; **911**, brick, 2 stories, gable roof, remodeled facade with corbelled cornice and doorway, early 19th C.; **917**, brick, 3 stories, ell, shed roof, bracket cornice, mid 19th C.

Also, **1007**, clapboard, 2 stories, gable roof, early 19th C.; **1009**, clapboard, now bricktex, 2 stories, gable roof, probably early 19th C. **1325**, brick, 2 stories, shed roof, bracket cornice, mid 19th C.

119. Built around 1815 by John McCobb, who also built 803 Prince.

302. Dates from ownership of Abijah Janney, 1826–1841. When sold to Thomas Semmes in 1842 it contained ten rooms. In 1849 purchased by Caleb Hallowell, nephew of Benjamin Hallowell, who enlarged it and established a school. By 1859 a three-story brick, forty rooms, with observatory, conservatory, and verandah. In November 1888 Richard Carne purchased it for St. John's Academy, advertised as having "educated over fifteen hundred boys and men, represented by twelve States and Territories," and as "one of the few military schools in the United States" with "tents and other camp equipage to go into camp every year."

Also, **121**, brick, small square building, low hip roof, office to 803 Prince, early 19th C.; **211**, clapboard, gable roof, probably early 19th C., remodeled.

112. Probably dates from brick carriage house and stable for 711 Prince, mentioned in the 1811 deed of James Patton to William Fowle. In the 1867 partition of Fowle's estate, conveyed, with land adjoining on the north, to William Fowle Dennis.

111. Built by Charles Bennett, who bought the lot in 1810. Probably Benjamin F. Price, who purchased it in 1865, added the Victorian embellishments. Price was the architect for the Corn Exchange building, today 100 King.

217. Built by David Ross around 1814–1820.

213. There was a frame house on the lot when John T. Evans bought it in 1856. Present house probably dates from Evans' ownership.

209. On January 1, 1798, John Dundas, Abraham Faw and Francis Peyton conveyed Commerce Street to the Mayor and Commonality of Alexandria for five shillings. The plat showing Commerce and adjacent streets is inserted at the end of Alexandria Deed Book K (Circuit Court) in connection with a deed of partition executed September 12, 1805, by Francis Peyton and John Dundas.

The house at 209 was probably built by Catherine A. Coakley, who bought the lot in April 1853. It remained in the Coakley family until 1942.

Also, **308**, clapboard, 2 stories, shed roof, front parapet; **310**, brick, 2 stories, shed roof, ell, bracket cornice, window heads; both probably mid 19th C.

It was "with the view to promote the interest and convenience of the inhabitants of the said Town of Alexandria," that Dundas, Faw and Peyton conveyed "a certain street called Commerce Street extending across their land." The deed, in defining the boundaries of Commerce Street, refers to the "east corner or butment of the new Stone bridge lately erected in Duke Street across Timber branch." The boundaries of the street, and additional information on the site of the stone bridge, are given in notations made by George Gilpin on the plat:

I do certify that Commerce Street is laid down on this plat agreeable to, and that it has expressly the location, as that plat had which was made when the deed was passed from John Dundas, Abraham Faw and Francis Peyton to the Mayor and Commonalty of the Town of Alexandria which deed bears date the first day of January 1798 and was admitted to record the seventh day of May 1798 and recorded in the records of the late Court of Hustings, Liber M, folio 347.* For the particulars of the location of Commerce Street reference may be had to the following remarks. Given under my hand June 1st, 1805. George Gilpin

REMARKS

At 38 Ft. 10 In. westward from the intersection of the south side of King Street with the east line of Fayette Street, the east line of Commerce Street intersects King Street, from this point it is 92 feet measuring with the south line of King Street to the west side of Commerce Street.

At 559 feet from the west side of West Street along the north side of Duke Street, the east side of Commerce Street intersects Duke Street this point of intersection is 125 eastward of the Wall or Butment of the Bridge.

Commerce Street is 50 feet in width.

Scale 50 feet to the Inch.

June 1st, 1805.   George Gilpin

In an 1841 advertisement heirs of John Dundas offer to sell property at the southwest corner of King and Commerce, describing this site as the "old diagonal pump corner." Both the stone bridge and the diagonal pump are mentioned frequently in early Alexandria newspapers as well-known points of reference.

* The correct deed book reference is K (Hustings Court), page 345.

DUKE

125, 123. In 1819 Richard Rock purchased the site of 125, 123 and 121. In April 1854 the lot was divided and sold. Elias Kincheloe paid $800 for the site of 125 and 123. A two-story brick house was then on this lot. In August 1855 the *Alexandria Gazette* listed among buildings recently completed, "a fine three-story brick dwelling house on Duke and Water streets for Elias Kincheloe." When the United States Government sold it at auction in April 1864 for $1,500, the lot contained two brick dwelling houses.

In June 1755 the Town Trustees directed John Carlyle to build a town warehouse on Point Lumley at the foot of Duke. Six years later the Trustees agreed that Thomas Fleming "would have the liberty to build a warehouse under the bank of Point Lumley," Fleming to have "the sole use and benefit . . . for three lives, at an annual rent of five shillings," because of his "usefulness as a Ship Carpenter and his inclination to serve this Town to the utmost of his power."

121. Built by Richard Rock around 1820. He purchased this lot, and the lots of 123 and 125 in 1819. When the property was divided and sold by court order in 1854, Margaret Rock purchased this house for $4,000.

Also, **110**, brick, possibly originally frame, 2½ stories, late 18th-early 19th C., Victorianized.

211. In May 1790 David Henley, merchant, formerly of Alexandria, then living in New York City, bought the quarter block on which this house stands. The deed conveying the lot of 211 to Sathaliel Allen in April 1803 provided that it include "the whole of the dwelling house which stands upon the premises."

117, 115. In June 1796 Mark Butts bought the lot of 117, and Thomas Preston the lot of 115, each paying $500. Probably Preston, a house carpenter, built both houses. In 1801 he advertised to remind those who had borrowed saws and planes from him that it was "high time they were returned." In March 1808 Butts sold 117 to Preston for $2,000. Photograph taken November 1960. Houses restored 1968.

The brick mansion house of Richard Arell was on the lot, now vacant, adjoining 115 on the east.

109. When Ephraim Mills, trunk maker, purchased this lot from the heirs of Richard Arell in March 1801, he agreed to build, within two years, "a brick house of at least two stories . . . at least 20 feet by 30 feet, or to contain 600 square feet." By 1814 Horace Field owned the house, and his tenant was Richard Rock.

207, 205. Both may date from small early flounders. 207 was advertised for sale in 1853 as "the brick tenement occupied by T. Darley." 205 was described in 1822 as a "small brick tenement." Early owners of the lot of 205 were: David Arell, whose heirs sold it to James H. Hooe on April 23, 1811, for $400; John McCobb, who bought it for $500 on June 14, 1811; and Horace Field, who bought it for $650 on May 18, 1815.

201. Probably dates from "the house and lot formerly occupied by Alexander McConnell" advertised for rent in 1797 by R. T. Hooe. In a March 15, 1854 notice of public sale described as a "new two-story frame tenement, with gas fixtures."

200. Leven Powell purchased this corner lot when the quarter block was divided and sold in May 1787 by James Mercer, brother and heir of George Mercer. Tax records for 1788 show Michael Clark as Powell's tenant. Powell and George Johnston, Jr., drafted the Resolves adopted by the freeholders of Loudoun County in 1774. Powell served with the Virginia forces during the Revolution, as major and lieutenant colonel; as a member of the Virginia House of Delegates in 1779, 1787–1788; and of the United States House of Representatives 1799–1801.

202. An Alexandria flounder house that never acquired an addition fronting on the street. Built by William Mitchell, who bought the lot in 1795 for £100. Sold at auction in 1805 to Samuel Craig for over $2,000. Again sold at auction in 1809, when John Gardner Ladd was the high bidder.

206. Probably built by James Johnson around 1850. Replaced a frame house built around 1794 by George Coryell, son of Cornelius Coryell of Coryell's Ferry, New Jersey. Traditionally, the senior Coryell acted as Washington's guide in that area during the Revolutionary War.

210. Probably built by John Short, "Watch Maker," who acquired the lot in 1783 for an annual ground rent. In 1789 advertised for sale as a "lot of ground with a three-story brick house and excellent back building." Sold in November 1789 to John B. Murray for £234 and assuming payment of the ground rent. Murray conveyed, with another lot Murray had bought for £71-10-1, to James Craik, in October 1795, for £1,500. Craik, Washington's "compatriot in arms and old and intimate friend," lived here until 1809. He accompanied Washington on his mission to the French in 1754; served with Washington under Braddock in 1755; in 1770 went with Washington to survey lands along the Ohio and Kanawha rivers; served in the Revolutionary army as Surgeon-General and as Assistant Director General of the Hospital of the Middle Department; and was one of the three physicians attending Washington in his last illness. In 1785 Dr. Craik moved from Port Tobacco, Maryland, to Alexandria. By September 1809 Craik was living in Fairfax County and offering his town house for rent. Craik died February 6, 1814, in "the 84th year of his age."

212. Described in a 1796 insurance policy as John Dunlap's "dwelling house, built of wood, two stories high, kitchen in cellar," and valued at $2,500. When Dunlap died in 1806, his executor was bonded for $50,000.

DUKE

306, 308. Jeremiah Blowford purchased 306 in November 1811 for $333.33, and 308 in January 1805 for $250. In April 1850 A. D. Collinsworth bought both for $500, and probably enlarged them. In 1852 Collinsworth sold 306 for $1,000.

Also, **304**, brick, 3 stories, mid 19th C.

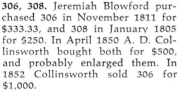

314, 316, 318. William Bushby may have built 314 (later Victorianized) and 316 in the late 18th century. By 1805 Samuel Adams owned 314. In 1802 John Horner bought the site of 316 and 318. In 1802 Horner sold 316 and 318 to John Constantine Generes, who for many years conducted a dancing school in Alexandria. When Generes advertised the property for sale in 1818, it contained the two-story brick house

Between 308 and 312 is **Chapel Alley.** The first Methodist Meeting House, a frame building, was on the west side of the alley, on a lot beginning 100 feet south of Duke, and extending west 43 feet and south 57 feet. This notice in an early Alexandria newspaper suggests that disputes developed during its construction:

Baltimore, June 19, 1794. The subscriber . . . does earnestly request all . . . kind people, who aided by their donations in building the Methodist Meeting House, while under his direction, to forward information in writing to Mr. William Hickman . . . his reasons for thus publicly making such a request are first: lest through hurry of business . . . he might have omitted giving credit for money, etc., received . . . ; secondly, . . . to convince a few censorious minds of his faithfulness to his trust, who have spared no pains . . . to injure him in his character . . . and quietly set down enjoying the fruit of another's labour and distress, without being willing to satisfy such just demands as are brought against them.

JAMES MORRISON

at 316, with adjoining brick buildings. When Generes conveyed 318 to Trustees of the First Presbyterian Church in July 1833, the deed referred to a one-story brick building.

325, 323, 321. Ephraim Evans, cabinet maker, bought the lot on which these houses stand in May 1794. His dwelling house is now 321. Thomas Davy bought the corner lot, site of 325–323, in 1832 for $200. In his will of July 15, 1876, Davy bequeathed to Thomas N. Davy of Ohio "the two frame houses standing at the corner of Royal and Duke." Photographed November 1960.

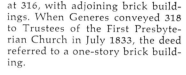

404. Built 1808–1809 and "finished in the handsomest stile" by Elisha Janney. Janney suffered financial reverses and the house was rented for some years. Early tenants were: Richard Bland Lee, 1811–1812; John Hopkins and his wife, formerly Cornelia Lee, 1813. Benjamin H. Lambert bought the house in 1853 and the doorway and vestibule probably date from his ownership.

Also, **408**, nucleus a one-story brick house owned and occupied by Dr. Elisha Cullen Dick in 1796. By 1853, or before, a three-story brick house. Home of Kate Waller Barrett when she died in 1925. Mrs. Barrett was active in establishing missions for unwed mothers, assistance to veterans, and in other charitable activities.

DUKE

414, 416, 418. Built around 1854. In February 1854 Benoni Wheat bought the lot of 414, and James F. Carlin purchased the lot of 416. William Baker bought the site of 418 in December 1853. In 1855 Baker pledged his lot, with the improvements thereon, as security for a debt of $5,000.

500. Built by Mary Mandeville around 1852, when she bought the lot for $700. Advertised in June 1864 as a "commodious two-and-a-half story brick dwelling house with metal roof." Purchased at auction by John P. Agnew for $4,275. Agnew owned a shipyard and numerous other Alexandria properties. Probably he added the mansard roof and Victorian decoration.

505. Until 1947 the site of this house was included in the lot of 501. When Maria Musgrove (later Maria Parsons) bought the property in 1836 the deed covered a brick house (501) and "all appurtenances." 505 was probably an "appurtenance."

501. Built by Peter Wise, who bought the quarter block on which it stands in 1778. By 1791 the owner was William Hunter, Jr., founder of the St. Andrew's Society of Alexandria, and mayor of the town 1787–1788, and 1790–1791. Hunter sold the house to George Augustine Washington, a nephew of General Washington. After George Augustine's death, his widow, Fanny Bassett, niece of Martha Washington, married Tobias Lear, then serving as Washington's secretary. In September 1795 Washington dined here with the Lears. Used as the Custom House by Charles Simms, Collector of the Port 1799–1819.

Also, **502,** brick, 3 stories, gable roof, sawtooth cornice, early 19th C.; **504,** brick, 3 stories, Greek Revival, probably mid 19th C.; **506,** brick, 3 stories, gable roof, antebellum type, mid 19th C.; **516,** brick, 2 stories, mid 19th C., extensively remodeled; **523,** clapboard with brick rear wall and brick cornice, shed roof with bracket cornice, nucleus probably early 19th C., major alterations mid 19th C.

518. The doorway of the dwelling house, "commodious in its plan and arrangement," built by Edward B. Powell in 1852. Contractors: J. W. Nalls & Bros., carpenters; Henderson & Bros., bricklayers.

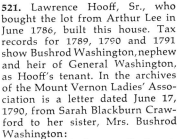

521. Lawrence Hooff, Sr., who bought the lot from Arthur Lee in June 1786, built this house. Tax records for 1789, 1790 and 1791 show Bushrod Washington, nephew and heir of General Washington, as Hooff's tenant. In the archives of the Mount Vernon Ladies' Association is a letter dated June 17, 1790, from Sarah Blackburn Crawford to her sister, Mrs. Bushrod Washington:

Your dinner I think was really elegant. 'pon my word Mrs. Washington you may thank me for having brought you to Alexandria. I think Bushfield and its environs was never intended for the sphere you (& your charming Washington) were made to move in.

519, 517. Probably built by Thomas Fitzpatrick, who bought the lot from Arthur Lee in June 1786.

515. Built by Matthew Robinson on a lot he bought in February 1797 from John D. Orr and his wife, the former Lucinda Lee. Arthur Lee, Revolutionary envoy and youngest son of Thomas Lee of Stratford, bequeathed the quarter block at the southeast corner of Duke and St. Asaph to his niece Lucinda, daughter of Thomas Ludwell Lee.

513. Enlarged and restyled, may date from "that two-story frame dwelling house lately built by Gurdin Chapin" mentioned in a 1797 deed. In 1793 Chapin married Margaret (Peggy) Reeder of Maryland. According to family historians, Peggy was a youthful sweetheart of William Wirt, who described her as "the most beautiful cherub God ever made." In 1807 Cephas Thompson painted the portraits of both Chapins. Chapin served as cashier of the Bank of Alexandria from 1800 until his death on June 26, 1811, when he was 46. His death notice paid him this tribute:

Our town has experienced the loss of no one who has left a wider chasm in society, and who has been more generally and sincerely lamented.

601. Described as "one of the choice examples of early American elegance in the United States," this house has suffered little from "improvements," or from the neglect that caused the deterioration of many of Alexandria's early buildings. After the Revolution Benjamin Dulany, son of the second Daniel Dulany of Maryland, moved to Alexandria and built this house. On February 21, 1785, Washington "Went to Alexandria with Mrs. Washington. Dined at Mr. Dulaney's." Benjamin married Elizabeth French, daughter of Daniel French of Rose Hill in Fairfax County, and a ward of Washington's. In the summer of 1799 the Dulanys purchased the house on

Shooter's Hill from Ludwell Lee. Thereafter they rented their town house until Robert J. Taylor bought it in 1810. Taylor was a leading lawyer and active in community affairs. Traditionally, it was from the steps of this house that Lafayette, on his visit in 1824, addressed the Alexandrians assembled to welcome him.

700. Built around 1820 by Jonathan Janney. In his will, signed March 12, 1838, Janney directed that all his real estate be sold, and that his wife receive

whatever balance may remain, if any, after the discharge of my just debts . . . entertaining great fear that there will be nothing as my losses and expenses arising in part from my long confinement from disease have been heavy.

Today the building is an encouraging example of the renovation and adaptation of an early building for commercial use.

706. Distinguished by its marble foundation and trim, its elaborate window heads and doorway, this antebellum house was under construction in June 1853, when the *Alexandria Gazette* reported:

The chimney of the gable end of the house being built for Mr. William Wallace Adam on Duke, above Washington, fell yesterday afternoon and caught Mr. George Richards, bricklayer, and two laborers, considerably injuring all of them.

William Wallace Adam was the grandson of James Adam (1755–1798) and the son of John Adam (1780–1843), both Alexandria silversmiths whose work is prized by collectors. William Wallace continued the family business.

805. May date from 1796, when William Cash, Jr., who purchased the lot in September 1795 for an annual ground rent, conveyed it to Amos Alexander for £100, Alexander to assume payment of the ground rent. Alexander served as mayor of Alexandria from February 1800 to February 1801. In July 1800 he conveyed this property, and the lot to the west, to Isaac Gibson for $950, in partial payment of a debt.

Also, **903**, clapboard, now bricktex, 2 stories, gable roof, probably early 19th C.; **904**, brick, 2 stories, bracket cornice, mid 19th C.; **907**, flush siding, 2 stories, salt box type, probably early 19th C.; **909**, clapboard and flush siding, 2 stories, gable roof, probably early 19th C.; **912**, brick front, clapboard sides now bricktex, gable roof, probably early 19th C.

801. This "large and well-arranged residence" under construction for Charles R. Hooff was listed in the *Alexandria Gazette* of April 3, 1852, among the current "Building Improvements." The contractors: B. H. Jenkins, carpenter; E. Francis, bricklayer.

Also, **802**, clapboard, re-sided, 2 stories, gable roof, mid 19th C.; **807**, brick, 2 stories above basement, wood sills and lintels, panels between windows, mid 19th C., restored 1974; **808**, clapboard, now aluminum siding, 2 stories, shed roof, nucleus flounder, mid 19th C. with late 19th C. additions and remodeling; **809**, clapboard, 2 stories, gable roof, mid 19th C., restored; **814**, brick, 2 stories above basement, cast-iron porch, mid 19th C., restored 1974; **825**, brick, 2½ stories, gable roof, end parapets, ell, false front, early-mid 19th C., reconstructed 1974.

DUKE

Also, **1001,** brick, 2½ stories, molded cornice, part gable roof with dormers, originally 2 units, early 19th C., being restored 1975; **1009,** brick, 2 stories, four bays wide, gable roof, areaway, mid 19th C.; **1017,** brick, 2 stories, gable roof, sawtooth cornice, probably early 19th C.; **1028,** brick, false front, 2½ stories, gable roof, parapets, ell, early-mid 19th C.

1123. Probably built by Alexander Veitch, who bought the quarter block on which it stands in April 1809. Sold at public auction, by court order, in July 1821. Thomson F. Mason was the high bidder at $855. The property had been appraised at $3,000.

1207. Built around 1809 by Charles LeCount Nevitt. Agnes Dundas, widow of John Dundas, was living here when she died May 23, 1820, "in the 50th year of her age." Her husband and her father, William Hepburn, were business partners. They prospered as Alexandria merchants and each acquired large holdings of local real estate.

1707. May date from ownership of John Longden, whose death "at his residence in West End," was announced April 1, 1830. In March 1844 Longden heirs conveyed it for $1,500 to Joseph Bruin. An 1853 insurance policy shows Bruin's two-story brick "Negro Jail," 42 by 32 feet, on this site. In July 1864 it was confiscated by the United States Marshal under the Act of Congress authorizing seizure of "the property of Rebels." Now offices.

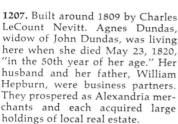

Also, **1211, 1209,** brick, 2 stories, shed roof, bracket cornice, window heads, areaway, double units, mid 19th C.; **1213,** brick, 2 stories, shed roof, bracket cornice, mid 19th C.

Also, **1621,** brick, 2½ stories, gable roof, single dormer, around 1820.

1315. Briefly the dwelling house (now much altered) of Robert Young, who built it around 1812 when he was Brigadier General of the Second Militia of the District of Columbia. The grounds covered the half block fronting on the north side of the 1300 block of Duke. Soon after the house was completed, Young met with financial reverses. In 1826 his former home was featured in this newspaper notice:

The Subscribers having leased for a term of years the large three-story brick house on Duke street, formerly occupied by General Young, we wish to purchase one hundred and fifty likely young negroes of both sexes between the ages of eight and twenty-five years.

FRANKLIN & ARMFIELD

For 33 years the house and grounds were used for what the deeds described as a "Negro Jail." A photograph taken when the Federal authorities were using it as a military prison shows that Price and Birch were the last proprietors.

FAIRFAX NORTH

Also, **221**, **219**, clapboard, 2 stories, mid 19th C.; **218**, brick, 2 stories, wooden bracket cornice, 19th C.; **216**, brick and clapboard, 2 stories, probably early 19th C.; **214**, clapboard, 3 stories, small windows on third floor, probably early 19th C.; **212**, clapboard, 2 stories, probably early 19th C.

208, 210. Described in a 1793 deed as "two brick houses belonging to and built by said William Duvall," who purchased the lot from William Ramsay on March 1, 1784. Charles Stier, son of Joseph Henry, Baron de Stier, was living in the house at 208 when it was advertised for rent in September 1799.

215, 213. Thomas Cruse built the house at 213 in 1815. Ten years earlier he was advertising Irish whiskey made last Christmas from malted barley. The few that have drank this Whiskey give it preference to Brandy. There is no doubt of it being a wholesome spirit.

In September 1833 Robert Jamieson bought the house and a vacant lot adjoining on the north; in 1851 he bought a third lot, also adjoining on the north. Jamieson then built the house at 215. After his death in 1863, both houses became the property of his son, Andrew Jamieson. Andrew Jamieson sold the property to Frank Corbett ten years later. Corbett divided the houses in 1882.

211, 209. Built by Jonah Thompson as two houses, the one at the rear with a loggia unique in North America. The documentary evidence now available suggests the house fronting on Fairfax was built around 1800–1805. If the house at the rear was built for Thompson's daughter Ann, after her marriage in 1812, it was probably the plan for the rear house that Benjamin Latrobe, writing Thompson on October 4, 1815, demanded be returned. Latrobe was annoyed by changes suggested by Thompson's "joiner." Thompson served as mayor of Alexandria March 1805–March 1808; succeeded William Herbert as President of the Bank of Alexandria; with Richard Veitch, at one time owned three of the "Six Buildings" in Washington, D. C. In 1850 Thompson's heirs sold the property to Benjamin Hallowell, who four years later conveyed it to his nephew, James S. Hallowell. In 1868 it became the first home of St. Mary's Academy.

207. A false brick front conceals an early clapboard house, home of John Dalton, a partner of John Carlyle. Carlyle and Dalton acted as Washington's agent in selling his tobacco and wheat. Dalton became a town trustee in 1750, and served for a time as Overseer of the town. In 1776 Dalton and George Mason of Gunston Hall built armed vessels, and procured arms, food and supplies for Revolutionary troops. Mason wrote Washington that he was "much obliged to the Board for joining Mr. Dalton with me. He is a steady, diligent man." In 1853 Dalton's great-granddaughter, Ann Pamela Cunningham, organized the Mount Vernon Ladies' Association, and as its first regent, conducted the successful drive for funds to purchase Washington's home.

201. Under construction when John Dalton died in 1777. Completed by his son-in-law, Thomas Herbert, who advertised it for rent as a tavern: a three-story brick corner house, shaped like an "L," having fronts on Cameron and Fairfax. A two-story kitchen, "the chimney ... conceived to admit a fireplace eight feet wide, with an oven on one side, and a set of fixed boilers on the other." On the lot a stable with twenty-eight stalls and a large carriage house. Washington came here to dine at "Mr. Lyle's new tavern" on September 26, 1785. Captain Henry Lyle died in April 1786. Succeeding tavern keepers were: George H. Leigh, 1787–1788; John Wise, 1788–1792; John Abert, 1794–1799; Peter Kemp, 1799–1800. Many dined here: Washington and other directors of the Potomac Company; the Alexandria Jockey Club; and in September 1798, the citizens of Alexandria, honoring John Marshall. At the Washington Birthnight Ball in 1791, "Joy beamed in every countenance. Sparkling eyes, dimpled cheeks, all the various graces of female beauty." In the early 19th century the tavern was converted into two dwellings. In 1814 Thomas Herbert was living in the corner house, and his son Noblett in the adjoining house. Served as the Anne Lee Memorial Home from 1916 until 1974.

133. The Bank of Alexandria was established by Act of Virginia Assembly in 1792. Construction of the banking house was begun in 1803. When completed in 1807, it was valued at $50,000. Fine interior woodwork remains. Above the banking room on the ground floor, with a ceiling fourteen feet high, spacious quarters were provided for the cashier and his family. The lot contained a smoke house and a stable. The bank failed in 1834. In 1848 James Green purchased the building and converted it into a hotel. Green made additions (now demolished) in 1855, and it was known as "Green's Mansion House Hotel." During the Civil War it was used as a hospital.

Until 1965, there were, in the half block adjoining City Hall on the south, two alleys, each 20 feet wide: one ran from Fairfax west to Royal on the southern boundary of the City Hall lot; the other began on the north side of King midway between Fairfax and Royal, and ran north to the other alley. On the southeast corner of the two alleys was a small double-flounder brick building. There is some evidence that the northern flounder, which had a fieldstone foundation, was originally the tavern of Richard Arell, mentioned in the diaries of George Washington from 1768 to 1774. Artifacts recovered from the site indicate the building was used as a tavern.

Carlyle House. East side 100 block. Built 1751–1753 by John Carlyle, a founding trustee and first Overseer of Alexandria. In 1755 he was appointed Major and Commissary of the Virginia forces. When General Edward Braddock and his troops arrived in Alexandria, Braddock and his staff took over Carlyle's house. On April 14, 1755, they met with the Council of Governors to plan the campaign against the French and Indians. Carlyle wrote his brother: "There was the Grandest Congress held at my house ever known on this Continent." On April 19 Braddock wrote Sir Thomas Robinson, one of His Majesty's secretaries of state, stressing "the necessity of laying a tax upon all his Majesty's dominions in America ... for reimbursing the great sums that must be advanced for the service and interest of the colonies in this important crisis." Ten years later Parliament passed the Stamp Act, and after its repeal, imposed other taxes that ultimately led the colonists to revolt. Carlyle served on the Fairfax Committee of Safety. His only son was killed at the battle of Eutaw Springs. Restoration by the Northern Virginia Regional Park Authority: architect, J. Everette Fauber, Jr. Admission fee.

115, 113. Built around 1796–1797 by Guy Atkinson. Itinerant artists established their studios in one of these houses: in the spring of 1805, Charles Fevret de Saint-Memin, and the following autumn, William Birch, who did portraits in enamel; in December 1805 and in May 1809, Cephas Thompson, portrait painter. These houses may have replaced an earlier house, probably frame, owned by Dr. William Ramsay, son of William Ramsay.

107. Built by Bernard Bryan on a lot he bought from Dennis Ramsay, son of William Ramsay, in 1795. In his will, signed February 6, 1841, Bryan bequeathed to his daughter Susanna "the house and lot on Fairfax street, my present residence, with all the furniture therein contained."

Southeast corner of King and Fairfax. In 1796 Colonel John Fitzgerald insured three frame buildings on the site of the Burke and Herbert Bank and Trust Company. One building may have been his "Counting Room" in which, on July 29, 1783, a young clerk "shqt himself through the head with a pistol," because "the unfortunate young man about two months before, had taken the measles, which left a gloomy depression on his spirit."

Also South, **109,** brick, 3 stories, replaced early frame building destroyed in January 1827 fire; **121,** brick, 3 stories, double sawtooth cornice, may date from 18th C. house of Peter Wise.

117. In September 1784 Robert Lyle offered to rent a "new Brick House . . . with eight rooms, Store, Kitchen, and Cellar under the whole . . . a convenient stable for four horses which may be easily converted into a warehouse." Nicholas Hannah advertised the opening of his coffee house here in December 1786, "with boxes and apartments." Tax records show James Craik was the occupant in 1788 and 1789. Probably renovated after January 1827 fire. Restored 1968.

107, 105. Stabler-Leadbeater Antique Shop and Apothecary Museum. The first bill of goods bought by Edward Stabler to stock his new shop in Alexandria was dated June 26, 1792. The site of his first shop is not known. By 1796 he was advertising as "Apothecary and Druggist" at 107, built by Philip Dawe, coppersmith, between 1774 and 1785. Dawe's tenants from 1787 to 1795 were Porter & Ingraham. On April 11, 1802, a note traveled from Mount Vernon to Mr. Stabler, Alexandria—Mrs. Washington desires Mr. Stabler will send by the bearer, a quart bottle of his best Castor Oil, and the bill for it.

Stabler bought 107 in 1805, and tradition says its slate roof saved it from serious damage in the January 1827 fire. In 1829 Stabler bought 105, probably built by John Watts on a part of a corner lot (70 feet on Fairfax, 40 feet on King) he bought in 1807. Stabler heirs extended the establishment north to King. When the shop closed in 1933, the Landmarks Society was organized to preserve it, and continues to maintain it. L. Manuel Hendler of Baltimore purchased the pharmaceutical equipment at auction in 1933, but permitted it to remain on loan, and in 1948 donated it to the Society. Open to the public.

41

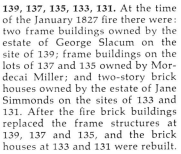

139, 137, 135, 133, 131. At the time of the January 1827 fire there were: two frame buildings owned by the estate of George Slacum on the site of 139; frame buildings on the lots of 137 and 135 owned by Mordecai Miller; and two-story brick houses owned by the estate of Jane Simmonds on the sites of 133 and 131. After the fire brick buildings replaced the frame structures at 139, 137 and 135, and the brick houses at 133 and 131 were rebuilt.

118, 120. Sites of both buildings bought by Bryan Hampson in June 1797. Between 1805 and 1815 a frame house on the double lot was replaced by a brick house. When offered for sale on January 8, 1827, the lot contained two three-story brick tenements, one used as a dwelling house, the other as a store and warehouse. George H. Smoot purchased both buildings in January 1838, and was living at 120 when he died in March 1870, aged 69. Smoot was the first president of the Orange and Alexandria Railroad, a director of the Chesapeake and Ohio and Alexandria Canal companies, president of the Bank of the Old Dominion, and of the Alexandria Water Company.

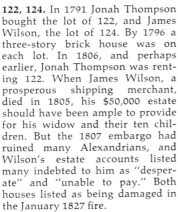

122, 124. In 1791 Jonah Thompson bought the lot of 122, and James Wilson, the lot of 124. By 1796 a three-story brick house was on each lot. In 1806, and perhaps earlier, Jonah Thompson was renting 122. When James Wilson, a prosperous shipping merchant, died in 1805, his $50,000 estate should have been ample to provide for his widow and their ten children. But the 1807 embargo had ruined many Alexandrians, and Wilson's estate accounts listed many indebted to him as "desperate" and "unable to pay." Both houses listed as being damaged in the January 1827 fire.

126. Now combined, offered for sale in April 1818 under a deed of trust executed by the "late Dr. James Kennedy, Jr.," as two lots "with distinctive tenements . . . part of which was formerly occupied by the deceased as a druggist's shop." Kennedy bought the lots in 1792 and 1795.

212. On March 23, 1786, Dr. William Brown announced that "The Medicine Shop kept by the Subscriber is moved to his new house on Fairfax Street." Dr. Brown served as Physician General in the Revolutionary army; as first president of the board of trustees of the Alexandria Academy, and as physician of the St. Andrew's Society of Alexandria. He is mentioned in Washington's diaries. He died in 1792, and it was his uncle, Dr. Gustavus Richard Brown of Maryland who was one of the three physicians in attendance at Washington's death. In 1800 Brown's widow offered to rent "That large and commodious house on Fairfax Street . . . having four good rooms and a garret, together with a good cellar. Adjoining . . . is a large brick kitchen, with two well furnished rooms over it . . . also a smoak house, stable and carriage house on the lot, and a pump of good water." Among Mrs. Brown's tenants were the widow of Colonel Richard Blackburn of Rippon Lodge; Carlyle Whiting, grandson of John Carlyle; and Judge William Cranch.

213. Built in 1812 by Reuben Johnston. In 1845 Johnston's heirs conveyed to Francis L. Smith, who was living here when he advertised the house for sale in May 1855. Smith moved from here to his new house at 510 Wolfe.

The building on the southeast corner of Fairfax and Prince was originally James Green's "extensive Cabinet Manufactory," completed 1836. It combined a three-story brick warehouse fronting over 98 feet on Fairfax, an adjoining brick building on the south fronting 16 feet on Fairfax, and replaced a three-story frame house adjoining on Prince. On the south wall the metal initials "J G" are used to terminate an interior supporting rod. Used as a military prison during the Civil War.

On the site of 216, 218, 220 there was, around 1800, a frame meeting house apparently built by the followers of Thomas O'Kelly, an early minister who left the Methodist Church to found a Christian sect. Early deeds refer to a graveyard on this lot. Dissenting members of the Episcopal Church used the meeting house from around 1807 until St. Paul's Church was completed in 1817. In 1818, dissenting members of the Presbyterian Meeting House established the Second Presbyterian Church, and used the meeting house until around 1840.

Also, **201**, brick, 2 stories, central chimney, possibly rear wing of mid 19th C. house at 300 Prince; **217**, clapboard, 2½ stories, built by Dr. William Baker c. 1786; **227**, brick, 3 stories, completed 1852 for George Plain.

209, 207. In May 1787 John C. Kempff announced that he had "removed to the large Brick House on Fairfax Street opposite to Doctor Brown's." A 1796 insurance policy refers to the "brick house of Hollensworth" on this lot. In 1833, described as having recently been occupied by Evan F. Taylor's coachmaking shop. James Green bought it in December 1842, and in May 1866 conveyed it to his son, John W. Green, who converted the building into two residences. In June 1891 he gave the house at 209 to his daughter, Fannie Lee Kemper; in April 1892, the house at 207 to his son, J. Johnston Green.

203. May date from ownership of Jacob Cox (1775–1796). John Wood purchased the property in 1813, and it remained in his family until July 1889, when Wood's heirs sold it to Charles W. Duffey.

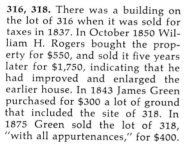

316, 318. There was a building on the lot of 316 when it was sold for taxes in 1837. In October 1850 William H. Rogers bought the property for $550, and sold it five years later for $1,750, indicating that he had improved and enlarged the earlier house. In 1843 James Green purchased for $300 a lot of ground that included the site of 318. In 1875 Green sold the lot of 318, "with all appurtenances," for $400.

323. Built by Charles B. Unruh around 1844. One of the ten early Alexandria buildings featured in Volume XII, Number 4, of *The White Pine Series of Architectural Monographs,* this unattached center hall dwelling offers a pleasant change from the town house facades of Alexandria's early streets. The wrought-iron on the entrance stairway is notable for its "lightness of scale, simplicity and delicacy."

Also, **302,** clapboard and composition siding, 2 stories, part mansard roof, mid 19th C. Victorianized and with later remodeling; **304, 306,** clapboard, 2 stories, false parapet, 2 units, late 18th-early 19th C.; **308,** clapboard, 3 stories, mid 19th C.; **310,** clapboard, 2 stories, false parapet, mid 19th C.; **312,** clapboard, 2 stories, mid 19th C.; **314,** clapboard, 2 stories, late 18th-early 19th C.

Presbyterian Meeting House. West side 300 block. In July 1773 Richard Arell and his wife conveyed the meeting house lot to William Thom, the minister, for "one shilling sterling money." On May 11, 1775, a notice, signed by John Carlyle and William Ramsay, appeared in the *Maryland Gazette*: "To be let to the lowest undertaker, the building of a brick church . . . sixty foot by fifty foot, and twenty-eight foot pitch." On October 18, 1790, "an elegant bell, cast at the foundry of Messrs. Morton & Foster, for the use of the Presbyterian Church of this Town" arrived from London, and it was announced that the "Congregation of that Church have it in contemplation to erect a handsome Steeple." The following January notice of a lottery to raise funds for the steeple appeared. On September 15, 1791, bids were requested: brick and stone work to be 95 feet high above the foundation, on which a wooden spire, 65 feet high, was to be erected. Tradition says that the bell rang from the time news of Washington's death reached Alexandria until after his funeral. On July 26, 1835, lightning struck the steeple, and the fire left only the walls and a part of the interior. The meeting house was rebuilt immediately according to the original plan. The present bell tower dates from 1843.

405, 403. James Lyle built the house at 405 on the lot he purchased from Mordecai Miller in June 1813 for $250. He sold the lot in 1831, "with a brick tenement thereon." Remodeled brick flounder house at 403 may be the "two-story brick tenement" mentioned in a March 1822 deed executed by Samuel Baggett, who bought the corner lot from Mordecai Miller in March 1816.

400. That part of the house fronting on Wolfe was built by John Wood around 1819. Renovated and substantially enlarged around 1967.

Also, **407**, clapboard and composition, 2 stories, gable roof, remodeled, probably mid 19th C.; **413**, clapboard, side composition, 2 stories, gable roof, brick ell, probably built by Laughlin Masterson c. 1812; **414, 416**, brick rear section, 2 stories, gable roof, areaway, double units, probably mid 19th C. (front section, shed roof, later); **415**, flush siding on front, 2½ stories, pilasters, arched treatment under porch, mansard roof, early-mid 19th C.; **417**, clapboard, 2½ stories, ell, probably early 19th C.; **423**, clapboard, 2½ stories, gable roof, dormer, probably 18th C. Victorianized; **418**, clapboard, 2 stories, gable roof, front altered, probably early 19th C.; **422**, clapboard, 3 stories over basement, Greek Revival, early 19th C.; **426**, clapboard, 2½ stories, gable roof, dormer, probably 18th C., restored.

410, 412. The house at 410, enlarged and Victorianized, may date from the ownership of John Hunter, who bought the lot in 1795. In 1852 Susanna Littlefield bought the property for $500 and in 1864 sold it to Thomas Hoy for $1,500. Victorian facade probably added by Hoy. Frame flounder house at 412 may date from ownership of Thomas Porter, and his wife Sarah, a daughter of William Ramsay, who bought the lot in 1798; or from ownership of Basil H. Davidson, to whom Porter's heirs sold it in 1815 for $360.

517, 515, 513, 511. Probably date from around 1817, when Joseph Milburn bought the lot of 517 and 515, and Levi Pickering purchased the site of 513 and 511. When Milburn's heirs sold 517 and 515 in 1834, the deed mentioned two brick tenements on the lot.

Also, **505, 507,** flush siding restored, 2 stories, gable roof, double units, early 19th C.

501. Built by Thomas Baird, who purchased 24 feet of the Fairfax street frontage in 1819, and the remainder at a tax sale in 1840. Remained in the Baird family until 1882. Renovated and restored.

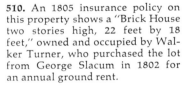

510. An 1805 insurance policy on this property shows a "Brick House two stories high, 22 feet by 18 feet," owned and occupied by Walker Turner, who purchased the lot from George Slacum in 1802 for an annual ground rent.

514. May date from "the wood house of Rebecca Greenway," widow of Joseph Greenway, referred to in a 1797 insurance policy.

Also, **601,** clapboard, 2 stories, probably early 19th C., restored; **603,** clapboard, 2½ stories, probably early 19th C., restored; **604,** clapboard, 3 stories, flat roof, small upper windows, Greek Revival, early-mid 19th C., **605,** clapboard, 2 stories, probably early 19th C., altered; **607,** clapboard, 2 stories, probably early 19th C.; **609,** clapboard with stuccoed end, 2 stories, probably early 19th C., altered; **611,** clapboard, 2 stories, probably early house Victorianized; **623,** clapboard, 2½ stories, 5 bays wide, center hall plan, gable roof, Greek Revival, mid 19th C.; **630,** brick, 2 stories, modillion cornice, probably early 19th C., remodeled.

Also, **719,** clapboard, 2 stories, gable roof, nucleus probably mid 19th C., altered; **725,** clapboard, 2 stories, shed roof, mid 19th C.

113 North. Probably built by Anthony Cazenove, who bought the lot in 1824 for $200, or by John D. Harrison, who purchased it from Cazenove in 1852 for $550.

114, 116 South. When Richard Stanton sold the house at 114 to Elijah Taylor in 1816, it was described as a "tenement and lot of ground." When Caleb Vernon conveyed 116 to James Harris in 1811, it was the "house and lot . . . occupied by the said Vernon." Under reconstruction in 1974.

Also South, **217,** clapboard, one story with rear shed, gable roof, probably mid 19th C.

814. Although early 19th century references to the race course indicate it was north and west of the town, some say this clapboard building (now brick veneer) was the pre-Revolutionary Jockey Club, and that horse races were held on a track at the rear. House may date from ownership of John Gill, who bought the square on which it stands in 1794, or from succeeding owners: Elisha C. Dick (1803); Robert Brown Jamesson (1804); Dr. Frederick May (1806). In 1817 James H. Hooe bought the house for $7,000.

North side 200 block. Contemporary stable of house at 619 South Lee.

Also, **211, 209,** brick, 2 stories with areaway, double units, probably early 19th C. 211 with additions, remodeled 1970.

414. Traditionally, "Spring Gardens," an early tavern where George Washington joined in the celebration of the Fourth of July in 1798. In 1818 William Yates purchased the quarter block on which it stands, and acquired additional land in the neighborhood. This section is today known as "Yates Gardens."

North side 800 block, site of "Arch Hall," bought in 1813 by Lawrence Lewis, nephew of George Washington and husband of Nelly Custis. A 1796 insurance policy described it as "one-story high, built of wood, 24 by 50 feet." The house was moved to Belmont Bay in 1950.

S.E. corner with Pitt. The photograph shows the house on its original lot at 109 South Pitt. Moved to present site October 1975.

William Fraser, in his will of November 9, 1825, bequeathed to his three daughters the "Brick Tenement and Lot of Ground I now own ... on the west side of Pitt street between King and Prince streets." Built either by Fraser, or by Jesse Taylor, who sold to Fraser in 1799 for 400 pounds, a price that suggests a building was then on the lot.

221. Early insurance policies indicate this house was built between 1815 and 1823, the lot then owned by heirs of Isaac Nichols of Loudoun County.

208. Probably built for Henry T. Thompson, who purchased the lot from Robert W. Hunter on April 9, 1840.

217. May have been built by Samuel Tucker who bought the lot at auction in 1844.

209, 207. Built before 1854 by William H. McKnight on the western part of the lot he purchased from John D. Johnston in 1831.

Also, **306, 308,** clapboard, 2 stories, shed roof, double units, probably mid 19th C., remodeled with additions 1958–1959.

Also, **514,** clapboard, 2 stories, gable roof, mid 19th C.; **518,** brick, 2 stories, gable roof, sawtooth cornice, early 19th C.; **522,** brick, 2 stories, dogtooth cornice, flounder type, early 19th C.; **524, 526, 528,** clapboard, 2 stories, gable roof, alleyway, probably mid 19th C., restored.

Also, **710, 712,** clapboard, 2 stories, shed roof, double units, probably mid 19th C., remodeled; **714,** clapboard, now bricktex, 2 stories, flounder type, probably mid 19th C.; **716, 718, 720, 722,** clapboard, now bricktex, 2 stories, gable roof, four units with alleyway in center, probably mid 19th C.; **723,** brick, 2½ stories, 3 bays, probably early 19th C., Victorianized.

Also, **819,** clapboard, now bricktex, 2 stories, gable roof, bracket cornice, mid 19th C.; **821,** clapboard, now bricktex, 2 stories, gable roof, bracket cornice, mid 19th C.

Also, **916,** clapboard, now bricktex, 2 stories, gable roof, bracket cornice, mid 19th C.

201. In 1797 Dennis McCarty Johnston, a sea captain and third son of George Johnston, Esq., purchased a large corner lot, around 103 feet on Lee, and 123 feet on Gibbon. In July 1831 Dennis' son, John D. Johnston, conveyed the Lee street frontage and 60 feet of the Gibbon street frontage to William H. McKnight. In November 1863 McKnight sold the corner lot with its present boundaries to Henry Baker for $230. House may date in part from McKnight's ownership.

119 Henry. Probably built by James Nutt shortly after he purchased for $200 in November 1808 a lot that included the site of this house. An 1829 advertisement described it as having "six good rooms, store room, kitchen, servant's room, etc." It was allotted to his daughter Elizabeth, wife of William F. Deakin, when Nutt's estate was settled in 1853.

214 Henry. Built by James Veitch 1817–1818. After several changes in ownership, this house, with other properties, was pledged in April 1857 to secure a debt of $60,000 owed by an Alexandria mercantile firm to Frederick S. Barreda and Company. When sold at auction in 1859, Barreda's bid of $525 was the highest. In May 1864 Barreda sold it to George H. Smoot for $2,500.

222 Jefferson. On June 3, 1801, Richard Libby, William Carne and Charles Slade purchased from William Thornton Alexander the half square on the south side of the 200 block. Two months later they divided the property, allotting the western two-thirds to Libby and Carne. Tax records show that Carne was living here in 1802. In 1811 Libby and Carne divided the real estate they owned jointly, and this house was given to Carne. In his will recorded January 28, 1812, Carne bequeathed it to his son, Richard Libby Carne, who, in 1832, offered for rent the "two-story Brick house and Clover Lot on the Mall, corner of Jefferson and Fairfax." A wing has been added on the east.

215 Jefferson. Built 1801–1802 by Joseph Dean, who in 1810 sold the house and the quarter block on which it stands to John D. Simms for $5,000. Four months later Simms, "being desirous of moving nearer to his office," offered it for rent, and in July 1811, for sale. In 1815 John Jackson bought the property, and a year later advertised to let "That elegant Establishment on Jefferson street, a commodious Brick dwelling, having Drawing, Dining, Store and five good Lodging Rooms, neatly finished—A Smoak House, Dairy, Kitchen, Stable, and every convenience. Pump under cover . . . a Garden well stocked with Vegetables." The addition on the west was completed in 1967.

JONES POINT

Jones Point Lighthouse. South and east of Lee and Green streets, on the Potomac. A fort was built on the point during the Revolution. It is shown on an unofficial 1803 map of Alexandria. The first cornerstone of the District of Columbia was installed on the point April 15, 1791. Specifications for the lighthouse were published August 27, 1855, and called for a frame building one and one-half stories high, on a brick foundation with basement, "having a circular tower on top for the support of the lantern, the horizontal dimensions being 38 by 19 feet." A month later the contract was awarded to C. B. Church of Washington, D. C., the building to be 19 feet high and the cupola 10 feet high. In May 1856 the lantern had been "elevated to its place," and was to be lighted "soon."

61

6. After spending the winter at Valley Forge, Colonel John Fitzgerald returned to Alexandria in the spring of 1778. That September the town trustees granted him and Valentine Peers the "sunken ground" on the south side of King east of Lee. By 1789, perhaps earlier, King had been filled in beyond Union. Today the facade of Fitzgerald's warehouses is much as it was advertised in 1801: "three brick warehouses, twenty-four feet four inches in front and three stories high . . . a Sail Loft above the upper story seventy-three feet in length and forty-two feet wide upon the floor . . . all under one roof." A modern wing has been added on the east. A visitor to Washington's camp in 1777 described Fitzgerald, an aide to the general, as "an agreeable broad-shouldered Irishman." He was Alexandria's leading Roman Catholic layman; one of the first directors of the Potomac Company; mayor from June 1786 to February 1787; commander of the Alexandria Independent Dragoons; and Collector of the Port. He died December 2, 1799. Seven military units marched in his funeral procession. His body was carried across the Potomac from Jones Point to Warburton Manor, and interred in the burying ground of the family of his wife, Jane Digges.

100. "The plan of the new Corn Exchange Building . . . handsomely executed by Mr. B. F. Price" was exhibited at an Alexandria store in the spring of 1871, the year it was constructed. It replaced three brick warehouses, built before 1796, purchased by the Federal government November 20, 1820, for use as a custom house.

Also, **112**, brick, 2 stories, early 19th C.; **128**, brick, 2 stories, early 19th C.

119, 117, 115, 113, 111, 109, 107, 105, 103, 101. Early warehouses, the majority dating from the late 18th or early 19th century, on land filled in by William Ramsay and his heirs. Early owners were: 119, James Patton and David Finley; 117, Benjamin Hamp; 115, James Wilson, Jr.; 109, William Yeaton; 107, Charles Page; 105, Hugh

Smith; 103, 101, Alexander Smith, John Dunlap and Andrew Fleming. In August 1800 Anthony C. Cazenove, agent for Victor duPont, son of Pierre Samuel duPont, purchased the warehouse at 117. The duPont's plan to trade in northern Virginia land was abandoned. The warehouse was rented until it was sold in 1807 pursuant to a deed of trust.

202, 204, built by Bernard Chequire, and **206, 208,** built by Colonel George Gilpin. With shops below and living quarters above, they combine commercial and residential use as they did when completed in 1798. Financial difficulties forced Chequire to sell 202–204 to Jonathan Swift in 1800. In 1820, perhaps earlier, the Union Bank was the occupant. Gilpin was the town's leading surveyor. His 1799 map of Alexandria, "handsomely engraven," has survived. Gilpin served in the Revolutionary troops, as a pall bearer at Washington's funeral, as first judge of the Orphans' Court of Alexandria, and as postmaster. He died December 23, 1813, "in the 73d year of his age." His obituary praised his "personal exertion towards the improvement of the town," and his "elevated and penetrating mind."

Also, **200,** brick, 3½ stories, built by Jacob Hoffman between 1802 and 1810; **210,** brick, 2 stories, built by John Ramsay around 1800.

221. Ramsay House. A 1956 reconstruction, based on early photographs, of the house of William Ramsay, a founding trustee of Alexandria. On November 30, 1761, at the Alexandria celebration of the Feast of St. Andrew, William Ramsay was elected Lord Mayor for the day: "an Honour doubly due him, as well for his Virtuous Desserts, as for being first Projector and Founder of this promising City. . . . A very elegant entertainment was prepared at the Coffee-House, where the Lord Mayor, Aldermen and Common Council dined. In the evening a Ball was given by the Scotch gentlemen. . . . The Night concluded with Bonfires, Illuminations, and other Demonstrations of Joy." Ramsay died February 10, 1785, in his 69th year. Washington walked in his funeral procession. Now Visitors' Center, headquarters of the Alexandria Tourist Council. Open to the public.

217, 215, 213, 211. Buildings at 217, 215 date from Hugh Smith's three-story brick warehouse, fronting on King 34 feet, built around 1803. Rebuilt after fire of November 17, 1855, in which seven Alexandria firemen were killed by a collapsing wall. In 1883 Henry Baader bought 217, 215, and a later building at 213. He purchased 211 in 1887. The 1877 Atlas of Alexandria shows three brick buildings of the same size at 217, 215 and 213, and a frame building at 211.

207, 205, 201. House at 207 built around 1810 by William Bartleman, who came to Alexandria in 1784, when he was fourteen. As Senior Deacon of Alexandria Washington Lodge No. 22, he walked in Washington's funeral procession. The brickwork of the small house at 205 appears to be early 19th century. Usually "alley" houses were not built until late in the 19th century. The building at 201 was "going up" for William Bayne on May 1, 1851. It replaced a large frame warehouse.

The 300, 400 and 500 blocks were cleared in the 1960's for urban renewal. By that time brick buildings dating from the early, mid and late 19th C. had replaced the earliest buildings, most of frame. On the north side of the 300 block were the Alexandria National Bank, the *Alexandria Gazette*, and the hardware store of Worth Hulfish. On the southwest corner with Royal was an 1829 brick building on the site of an earlier frame, said to have been the office of George Mason of Gunston Hall. Across the street, on the northwest corner with Royal, a brick building had replaced the early frame tavern of William McKnight. The first structure on the southeast corner with Pitt was a three-story brick built by John Dundas around 1785, and successively, the Washington Tavern, the Franklin House and the Marshall House. When Federal troops occupied Alexandria on May 24, 1861, Colonel Ellsworth of the New York Zouaves removed the Confederate flag flying over the Marshall House, and was shot dead by the proprietor, James Jackson, who was instantly killed by a soldier accompanying Ellsworth. This early building burned in 1872. Toward the center of the north side of the 500 block, concealed by an 1886 front, was the early 19th C. classic revival built for the Mechanics' Bank. On the south side of the 500 block were several early 19th C. buildings. One was occupied by Shuman's Bakery, for many years a popular luncheon and meeting place of downtown merchants and local officials.

629. Amos Alexander, mayor from February 1800 to February 1801, neatly "turned the corner" when he built this house on a lot he bought in 1799. Purchased in 1807 by Robert Young, who was Brigadier General in the District of Columbia militia during the War of 1812, President of the Mechanics' Bank, and Judge of the Orphans' Court of Alexandria. He met with financial reverses in 1817. In his will he called the loss of his money "trifling compared to the venom of evil toungs (sic) proceeding from bad hearts."

Also, **601**, incorporating old brick walls, on the site of the late 18th C. Indian Queen Tavern.

Also, **715**, brick, 3 stories, gable roof, early 19th C., major alterations; **717**, brick, 3 stories, gable roof, early 19th century.

713, 711, 709, 707, 705, 703. Probably built 1816–1817, by the following owners: 713, Charles Bennett, who was living here when he died in April 1839; 711, 709, Jacob Hoffman; 707, 705, John Withers; 703, Benjamin Baden. In 1825 William Washington bought 711, 709. In March 1866 his heirs, Maria and Anne Washington, sold it to Louis Appich.

Also, **805,** brick, 3 stories, shed roof, early-mid 19th C.; **806,** brick, false front, 2½ stories, gable roof, probably early 19th C.; **818,** brick, 3 stories, small upper windows, flat pitched roof, kitchen ell, mid 19th C.

923, 921, 919. Francis Peyton built 923 and 921 after 1797, when he acquired the quarter block on which they stand. In 1826 Peyton pledged them in a deed of trust. When Peyton conveyed the lot of 919 to William Gore in June 1805, for an annual ground rent, it was "to comprehend the brick house now erected by William Gore." In 1813 Gore sold 919 to Craven Peyton Thompson for $2,400.

917, 915. Built by William Myers between 1798 and 1802. In November 1803, Maria H. H. Rozier, widow of Francis Hall Rozier, purchased the house at 917. Four years later the widow and Dr. William A. Daingerfield entered into a marriage agreement, reserving to her the control of property she had inherited, including Notley Hall, across the river in Maryland. Dr. Daingerfield was the youngest son of William Daingerfield, of Belvidera, near Fredericksburg, and the brother of Bathurst Daingerfield. Myers sold 915 to John Mills in March 1803. Anthony C. Cazenove bought it in January 1816, and in his will referred to it as his "former dwelling house."

907. Originally two stories. Probably dates from house built by Benjamin Baden around 1805. In 1816 Anthony C. Cazenove bought it for $2,300.

Also, **910**, brick, 3 stories, false front, originally 2 stories, shed roof, originally gable roof, probably early 19th C.

900. May date from ownership of John Richter, who bought the site in 1796. After Richter's death, the corner lot, then fronting around 49 feet on King, including the "dwellings and warehouses thereon," was sold to Anthony C. Cazenove in November 1813 for $3,050.

Also, **1000**, brick, 3 stories, flat pitched roof, stepped ends, modillion cornice, rear ell, early 19th C. with alterations; **1021**, **1019**, brick false front, 2½ stories, gable roof, dentil cornice, probably early 19th C.

1011. Built by Ambrose White, who bought the lot from George Mc-Munn in December 1801 for payment of an annual ground rent. Four years later White sold it to Mark Butts for $1,375, Butts also to assume payment of the ground rent.

1007. Built around 1805–1806 by Bolitha Laws, a brick contractor who had a prominent role in rebuilding Fort Washington after its destruction during the War of 1812. Phineas Janney was the tenant 1812–1814. Anthony C. Cazenove bought it in July 1814 for $3,200. In 1856 Cazenove's executors conveyed the house to Sarah W. Griffith, a daughter of the Reverend David Griffith, an early rector of Christ Church. Restored 1970.

1010. Probably built by Jacob Hoffman, who bought the lot in 1811 for $505, and sold the property to Peter Hoffman of Baltimore for $1,250, in 1817.

Also, **1116**, brick, false front, 2 stories, gable roof, probably early 19th C.; **1117**, flush siding, 3 stories, shed roof, mid 19th C., altered; **1118**, brick, false front, 2½ stories, gable roof, probably early 19th C.

1102, 1104, 1106. On a quarter block William Thornton Alexander conveyed to William Rhodes in 1797. House at 1102 built either by William Lanphier, around 1805, or by Benjamin Baden, around 1810. Houses at 1104 and 1106 may have been built by Joseph Smith, who bought the lots in 1811.

1120, 1122. Built around 1803–1804 by William Myers who bought the site in 1803 for £50 and sold the property to William S. Moore in 1813 for $1,700.

1201. May date from a brick building Thomas Preston agreed to build on this corner lot in May 1808. By December 1837, John D. Harrison was the owner. It was owned by Harrison's heirs until 1895. In the 1880's, known as "Cox's Hotel and Wagon Yard."

Also, **1211-1207**, brick, false front, 2 stories, gable roof, double units, probably early 19th C.; **1212**, brick, 3 stories, gable roof, mid 19th C., altered; **1214**, brick, 3 stories, gable roof, mid 19th C.; **1216**, **1218**, brick, 3 stories, shed roof, double units, mid 19th C.; **1225**, brick, 3 stories, originally 2 stories, probably early 19th C., major alterations; **1229**, brick, 3 stories, originally 2 stories, probably early 19th C., major alterations and additions.

1300, 1304. House at 1300 built by Benjamin Baden, who bought the lot from John McKinney in March 1813 for $720, and sold it in October 1814 to Bernard Bryan for $2,000. House at 1304 apparently built for Ann Peyton, to whom the lot was conveyed for $1 in 1800 on the understanding that she would "erect a brick house thereon." In July 1805 Ann and her husband, Francis Peyton, sold it to John McKinney for $1,000.

1325. In November 1819 James Sanderson pledged this "two-story brick warehouse" and other property in a deed of trust. Probably built by Sanderson after he purchased the lot from William N. Mills in 1808.

1317. Probably built by James Sanderson after 1808 when he bought frontage on King extending from Payne east 101 feet. When sold to Francis Peyton in January 1835 for $600, described as a "brick dwelling house."

1322. Probably built by the senior Francis Peyton in the early 1800's. In February 1843 his son and namesake conveyed this lot of ground to Edward Burchell, "upon which lot a brick store and dwelling house is erected, now occupied by Robert House, which lot was allotted to the said Francis Peyton by Commissioners as a part and portion of his interest in the estate of Colonel Francis Peyton, the elder, deceased."

1222. May date from ownership of Gilbert S. Minor who bought the lot in October 1853, and sold in November 1854 for $1,500. Probably renovated and restyled by George Bauer, who purchased it in 1875 for $850. Sold at auction by court order in 1910 for $6,000.

Also, **1305**, brick, 2 stories, gable roof, modillion cornice; mid 19th C.; **1313**, brick, false front, 2½ stories, early-mid 19th C.; **1321**, brick, 2½ stories, gable roof, molded cornice, early 19th C., altered.

On the hill dominating King stood, in 1784, the "Mansion-House" of John Mills, "well-known for its beautiful Situation, and the absolute Perfection of the Plan." By 1797 Ludwell Lee, son of Richard Henry Lee, was the owner. In 1799 Lee sold it to Benjamin Dulany. Civil War photographs show Fort Ellsworth and Federal troops on the hill. Today the George Washington National Masonic Memorial, built 1922–1932, provides a view of the present and a link with the past. Among the exhibits are numerous Washington memorabilia, including a replica of the lodge room of Alexandria Washington Lodge No. 22, and the chair used by Washington when he presided as Worshipful Master. Open to the public.

113. Lawrence Washington, half brother of George, purchased the quarter block on which this house stands at the first auction of lots in July 1749. Joseph Riddle and his partner, James Dall of Baltimore, purchased the site in November 1801. On November 30, 1803, Riddle advertised this "two-story brick house, completely finished," for sale or for rent. Samuel B. Larmour purchased Riddle's half interest in 1816, and Dall's in 1818.

107 (rear). The brick building at the rear (may be seen from the alley) was the stable of the house today 202–204 King. Jonathan Swift purchased this lot, and the lot of the building today ½ Swift Alley, in January 1802 for $960.

116, 118, 120. When the lot of 116 was sold in 1851 to settle the estate of Joseph Mandeville, it contained a soap factory. A deed of trust executed by Edward Sheehy in 1833 says Sheehy was then operating the factory as Mandeville's tenant. The factory may have been remodeled for residential use, or replaced, after it was conveyed to the heirs of Samuel Lunt in 1853. Sheehy purchased the lots of 118 and 120 from heirs of John Harper in 1825 for $210 each. The house at 118 sold for $705 at public auction in 1849. In 1847 George H. Markell bought the house at 120 for $850.

106. In 1789 John Fitzgerald conveyed the lot of 106 (including "a part of the wharf made by him") to John Jenckes, Olney Winsor and Joseph Jenckes. By 1793 the lot contained a "new three-story Brick Warehouse." In 1798 it was Daniel McLean's "Bake-House." Andrew Jamieson and Robert Anderson bought it in 1802, and continued the bakery for a time. In 1818 it was "the Armory." Probably converted to residential use in the 1930's.

The early brewery of Andrew Wales was on the north side of Wales Alley, on the Potomac. At the time the river extended farther west than it does today.

225, 223. In 1795 the heirs of David Arell conveyed to Alexander McConnell, for an annual ground rent of $150, the land on which these houses, and the house at 201 Duke, stand. A later deed refers to these houses as having been "erected by Alexander McConnell."

221. Built by Absalom Wroe, to whom the lot was conveyed in January 1794 for an annual ground rent. In October 1802 Wroe sold it to John McCobb for $850, McCobb to assume payment of the ground rent. After several changes in ownership, sold at public auction on September 15, 1832. The highest bidder, at $395, was George W. D. Ramsay, son of Captain Dennis Ramsay and grandson of William Ramsay, a founding trustee of Alexandria. The following January Ramsay conveyed it to his brother Robert T. Ramsay, in trust for the use of their sister Ann, widow of Robert S. Blacklock.

209. A plat on an 1817 insurance policy covering the Farmers' Bank (southwest corner Lee and Prince) shows "Lawrence Hill's brick house" on the lot of 209. Hill bought the lot in 1814 for $1,400, and sold it fifteen years later for $2,250. After several changes in ownership, Francis M. Hill purchased it in 1884, and probably Victorianized the house.

219. In July 1783 David Arell conveyed the lot, for an annual ground rent, to Lewis Weston, ship carpenter. Weston died in 1795, and bequeathed to his wife Mary a frame house on the lot of 217, and directed that the "brick house adjoining the frame house" be sold. A deed relating to 221 indicates that a brick house adjoined it on the north. In August 1807 Weston's son conveyed 219 to Anthony Dyer for $1,235, Dyer assuming payment of the annual ground rent.

217. Elizabeth Monroe bought the property in 1844 for $370. Probably she replaced an early frame dwelling on the lot built by Lewis Weston. Elizabeth and her heirs owned the house until 1917.

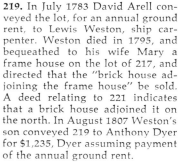

207, 205, 203. In March 1811 the heir of Robert Townshend Hooe conveyed these buildings, and the building adjoining on the north (now 201 South Lee and 200 Prince) to the Farmers' Bank of Alexandria. In July 1847 this bank became a branch of the Exchange Bank of Norfolk, and the Alexandria bank deeded the property to the Exchange Bank. In July 1867 the First National Bank of Alexandria acquired the property, and in December 1909 sold it to Robert P. Aitcheson. When it was sold in January 1918 it was described as "those five brick houses with the land upon which the same are located . . . known as 200 Prince, and 201, 203, 205, and 207 South Lee street."

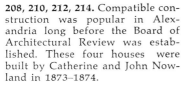

208, 210, 212, 214. Compatible construction was popular in Alexandria long before the Board of Architectural Review was established. These four houses were built by Catherine and John Nowland in 1873–1874.

218. Probably built around 1844 by George Brown. In July 1876 David L. Smoot advertised as "A GREAT BARGAIN . . . that excellent Brick Dwelling House . . . in which I am now living . . . fourteen rooms and most of the modern conveniences, such as hot and cold water, gas, bath room and water closet, heaters, kitchen range, etc. Upon the lot . . . is a frame stable, wood house, some fruit trees, vines, etc."

224. According to family tradition, incorporates early buildings erected around 1757 by George Johnston, Sr., and around 1772 by his son-in-law, Robert Hanson Harrison. Daniel Douglass bought the property around 1800, and was in

220. Sold to Adam Douglass in 1797 for £521, suggesting that a building was on the lot. In 1829 it sold for $700, "with the buildings and improvements thereon." Purchased for $1,000 in 1840 by Thomas Burns, who sold it in 1858 for $1,500.

turn enlarging the house when he died in 1803. His improvements were completed by Thomas Vowell. George Johnston, Sr., an attorney, represented Fairfax County in the House of Burgesses. In 1765 he joined Patrick Henry in advocating the adoption of the resolutions on the Stamp Act. Johnston was also a trustee of Alexandria. After he died in 1766 his friend, George Washington, succeeded him in the House of Burgesses and as a town trustee. Johnston's son and namesake served as an aide to Washington from January 20, 1777, until his death from camp fever at Morristown, New Jersey, on May 29, 1777. Many of his letters to friends have survived, evidence of his charm and ability. Robert Hanson Harrison, a native of Charles County, Maryland, was clerk of the Fairfax County meeting at which the Fairfax Resolves were adopted on July 18, 1774. On May 16, 1776, he was appointed secretary to General Washington, and served until the end of the war.

325. Built by Mark Mankin after he bought the lot of 325 and a lot adjoining on the south in 1848. The division into two lots was made when Mankin's estate was settled in 1904.

321, 319, 317. House at 321 probably built by Josiah H. Davis, who bought the lot in December 1823 for $180. When Davis pledged in a deed of trust in January 1850, it was described as a "tenement and lot of ground." 319 and 317 may date from the ownership of Jeremiah Dowell, who bought the land in December 1820. In July 1865 Albert H. Dowell sold 319 to Joseph W. Denty for $775. In 1857 317 sold for $425.

311. Conveyed in June 1855 by heirs of George Slacum to Ebenezer Bacon for $750. The price suggests that the lot, conveyed to Slacum in 1787, had been improved. In 1874 Joseph Hopkins paid $500 for it, and in 1883 sold it for $1,500. Probably the house was renovated during Hopkins' ownership.

315. Built by Ebenezer Bacon around 1851–1852. In June 1851 Nehemiah Hicks and his wife Betsy, a daughter of Henry Bayne, conveyed a "vacant lot of ground" to Bacon and his wife Susan, also a daughter of Henry Bayne, for $1.00, in a partition of Bayne's estate. In August 1887, William H. Bacon, Special Commissioner, conveyed this house, and the house at 317, for $1,500.

313. Probably built by Thomas Greenleaf, who bought the lot in February 1822. When Greenleaf's sister and heir conveyed it to Ebenezer Bacon in August 1847, described as a "tenement and lot of ground."

307. The brick stable at the rear was built either by John B. Murray, who acquired the lot in 1787, or by Dr. James Craik, who in October 1795 bought it from Murray with the house at 210 Duke. Dr. Craik's heir conveyed the stable and lot to James Brooks in November 1830 for $250. The brick house was built by Brooks, who in January 1834 sold the property to Robert H. Murdoch for $1,300.

310. When Robert T. Hooe and Richard Harrison conveyed this lot to John Muncaster in 1796, the deed mentioned a "house thereon built by James Grimes." A house may have been on the lot when George Chapman sold it to Hooe and Harrison in 1790, because they conveyed it to Muncaster for the same price they had paid. By 1805 Muncaster had acquired a yard and garden adjoining on the south. An 1805 insurance policy covered a two-story wooden dwelling house, 20 by 30 feet, valued at $1,500, and a kitchen and stable. Muncaster married a grand-daughter of Richard Arell, an early Alexandria innkeeper.

314, 316. Built around 1851–1852 by Benjamin H. Jenkins who bought the land on which these houses stand in March 1848 for $200. Three years later he pledged the lot, including "the buildings thereon erected and to be erected," in a deed of trust. In April 1858 Jenkins sold 314 to Thomas E. Kemp for $800, and 316 to William Buckingham for $700.

318. In February 1860 Benjamin F. Price agreed to build a house on this lot for Annie Crump, "to cost about the sum of $1,200."

320, 322. Probably built around 1853 by Frederick Miller, who bought a 40 foot frontage on Lee in 1850, and an additional 6 feet 5 inches in 1853. In 1887 Miller's heirs conveyed to Dorothea Appich "with the buildings thereon situated."

328, 330. Probably built or enlarged by George Swain, who bought the 50 foot frontage on Lee from Hugh Smith in two transactions: the 20 feet on the corner in November 1845 for $250, and the 30 feet adjoining on the north in December 1851 for $375. Each lot then extended 100 feet to the east. The deeds mention "appurtenances." In 1871 Swain heirs conveyed the lot as it is today (50 feet by 50 feet) "with improvements" for $850.

435, 433. Both may date from the ownership of William Wright, who acquired the land in 1792 for an annual ground rent. In 1816 Wright sold to John Hunter for $800, Hunter assuming payment of the ground rent. In May 1850 Margaret Dyer, Hunter's daughter, sold 435 to John S. Ratcliff for $250, and 433 (with a lot on Wilkes) to John Thomas Hill for $360.

429. May date from a house on the lot when Jacob Cox conveyed it, and other land, to John C. Vowell in 1800 for $2,000. When Vowell pledged it in a deed of trust in 1806, the deed referred to a "tenement and lot of gound."

419. Dates from early house of James Keith, who bought the lot of 419 and 421 in July 1783. Early tax records show a frame house on the lot. The stone foundation of a part of the present house suggests that it is on the site of the early dwell-ing. On Tuesday, June 27, 1797, an Alexandria newspaper announced: "General John Marshall, of the extra embassy of the United States to the French Republic, passed through this town last Sunday." Three days earlier Marshall wrote his wife that he was "now at my uncle Keith's, where everybody treats me with the utmost affection and friendship." "Uncle Keith" was a brother of Marshall's mother. He was mayor of Alexandria in 1784, and President of the Potomac Company from 1798 to 1807. He was a frequent visitor to Mount Vernon. He died in October 1824, "in the 90th year of his age." The house remained in the Keith family, who probably replaced the frame with the brick dwelling, until March 1861, when Ezekiel Jones bought it for $650. In 1884 Jones sold it to Annie L. Moore, widow, for $1,400. The increase in price indicates that Jones had renovated and enlarged the house. Mrs. Moore conveyed the house, with its present lot, to John M. Johnson in October 1896.

427, 425. Built around 1853. House at 427 by John S. Ratcliff, house at 425 by Stephen Swain, each purchasing his lot for $175 from Andrew Jamieson in March 1853. In July 1855 Ratcliff sold 427 to George C. Hewes for $825. In March 1894 Swain sold 425 to Richard Nalls for $550.

423. May date from ownership of either John Saunders, who bought the lot in November 1784, or of Theophilus Randall who purchased it from Saunders' executors in September 1796 for £100. When Randall conveyed it to John Roach for $450 in August 1823, the deed covered "a tenement and lot of ground." In March 1851 William Joseph Mills bought it from Roach's son for $600, executing a deed of trust which was not released until February 1874.

417. Probably built by John Jamieson who in May 1839 bought the lots of 417 through 411 for $85. 417 sold to James Fadely for $500 on August 1, 1851. Fadely sold in 1858 for $800.

415, 413. Among the "Building Improvements" listed in the *Alexandria Gazette* of April 3, 1852, were these "large and handsome frame buildings for W. Markley, the work done by himself." The roof of 415 has been raised.

LEE SOUTH

411. May date from the ownership of Samuel Montgomery Brown, to whom Thomas Fleming conveyed in 1783, for an annual ground rent, the land on which the houses at 411 through 417 stand. In February 1802, Fleming heirs repossessed, having unsuccessfully tried to collect overdue ground rent "at the Front Door of the Dwelling House erected upon said premises." After several changes in ownership it was sold in 1850 to William H. Markley for $500.

407, 405, 403, 401. Possibly 407 dates from ownership of an heir of Thomas Fleming, a grandson who in February 1798 pledged the lot of 407 (and 409), "with all appurtenances," as security for a debt of $1,201. A later deed indicates 407 pre-dated 405. House at 405 built by Charles Fadely, who bought the lot in 1846 for $155, and sold it in 1852 to James Fadely for $700. House at 403 may have been on the lot when Thomas Patten sold it to William Milnor, Jr., in 1797 for £96. In 1799 John Haine (Hein) bought it for £90, and in 1801 sold to John Guthrie for $306. In October 1802 Guthrie conveyed the house and all its furnishings, including his "Coat of Arms," to his two daughters. Harriet Jackson, an heir of Thomas Fleming, sold the lot of 401 to Samuel Bartle for $225 in September 1812. In 1818 Bartle pledged this "tenement and lot of ground" in a deed of trust. Andrew McClean of Fortress Monroe bought it in 1820 for $4,000.

LEE SOUTH

402, 404, 406, 408, 410, 412. Built by Emanuel Francis, who in October 1846 purchased the lots of 402 and 404, and in April 1849, the lots of 406, 408, 410 and 412. Francis sold the lot of 404 to Elihu Mankin in 1848 for $80, and it remained in the Mankin family until 1919. In January 1869 Francis sold the "tenement and lot of ground" at 402 to George W. Mankin for $1,325.

Lot of 414 site of an early brick schoolhouse built by Archibald McLean. In August 1813 McLean conveyed it to Bushrod Washington and Lawrence Lewis, acting Executors of the estate of George Washington "in consideration of the sum of ——— (sic) paid to him by the said George Washington in his lifetime."

428, 430. May date from ownership of Hugh Smith, who at a tax sale in 1840 purchased a lot which included the sites of these houses. In 1878 Smith's executors sold this lot and additional Lee street property on the north to Elvira Hill, wife of John T. Hill.

Also, **421**, clapboard, 3 stories, small upper windows, areaway, early 19th C.

418, 420. House at 418 completed in the spring of 1787 by Daniel Roberdeau on a part of a lot he bought in 1774. During the Revolution Roberdeau was a member of the Pennsylvania Committee of Safety, and in 1777, a delegate to the Continental Congress. In September 1785 Roberdeau's daughter married Jonathan Swift, a leading citizen and merchant of Alexandria. Roberdeau's son Isaac was chief assistant to L'Enfant. In November 1792 Roberdeau advertised his house for rent: "28 feet 4 inches in front, 40 feet deep, and three stories high . . . with a kitchen and smoke-house . . . a yard, stables and carriage house." An Alexandria newspaper of November 22, 1795, announced the sale of household furnishings "at the late dwelling of General Roberdeau, deceased, in Winchester, Virginia." Recently renovated and restored. House at 420 dates from an early outbuilding of 418. In 1840 Hugh Smith purchased a lot, of which the lot of 420 was a part. In April 1871 Smith's executors conveyed 420 to John Aitcheson for $530, granting use of "a portion of the lot north of the said lot 44½ feet long by 9 inches wide, where the wall of the house now standing . . . extends over the line of said lot on the north, so long as the present wall shall remain standing and no longer."

531. May date from ownership of William H. McKnight, who in 1831 bought a lot of ground of which the site of this house is a part. McKnight sold to C. R. Van Allstyn in 1865 for $180 "cash." Van Allstyn probably renovated the house before he sold it to W. P. Graves in April 1868 for $800.

529, 527, 525, 523. Built by William H. McKnight on a part of a lot of ground he bought for $300 in 1831. In 1852 he pledged them in a deed of trust. Advertised in 1866 as "Four frame houses . . . each containing six rooms."

521, 519. In 1796 Alexander Veitch acquired the lots of 521 and 519 for an annual ground rent. In 1798 Veitch sold the lot of 521 to Christian Ludwick Hebrigle, then of Bladensburgh, Maryland. House at 521 probably built by Hebrigle. In his will, recorded January 2, 1819, Hebrigle bequeathed everything to his wife, and after her death, to his six children. Owned by his heirs until it was sold in November 1865 for $683. Veitch probably built the house at 519 before he sold the lot in 1803 to George Noble Lyles for $1,125, Lyles to assume payment of the ground rent.

513, 511. In 1787 William Hunter, Sr., conveyed the land on which these houses stand to Peter Bohrer for £259. In March 1797 Bohrer sold to Robert Miller for £400. The increase in price suggests that Bohrer had built on the lot. Miller sold to Jane H. Slacum in 1815. Four years later Mrs. Slacum sold a house and the present lot of 513 to Hannah Gird for $1,200, "reserving . . . the right of arching over" an alley then running along the north side of 513, "whenever a building is erected on the lot to the north of said alley." In September 1850 John Heymes bought 513 for $1,000, and in November 1853, the lot of 511 for $275. Presumably Heymes enlarged and restyled 513, and built the house at 511.

509. Built by Captain John Mc-Namara 1811–1812. In 1812 Mc-Namara was the occupant; in 1816, Ebenezer Vowell; in 1817, William Wood.

505. Tax records for 1802 list a frame house on this lot, owned by William Hunter, Sr. Advertised in January 1811 as a "good two-story framed dwelling house." John Hunter, whose early shipyard was on the Potomac between Wolfe and Wilkes, bought it in July 1811. Later Hunter's son Robert lived here, and as Alexandria's "indefatigable and accomplished Naval Architect," took over the shipyard. In 1869 Robert's son Joseph, then living in the house, sold it to John W. Burke, one of the founders of the Burke and Herbert Bank and Trust Company. Burke's second wife was a great-grand-daughter of Thomas Jefferson. Her father, Nicholas P. Trist, was appointed postmaster in Alexandria in 1870, and is said to have lived here until his death in 1874. House probably restyled by Burke.

619. Built around 1800 by Thomas Vowell, Jr., a prominent Alexandria merchant. Advertised for sale in September 1817, the house was "28 feet front and 40 feet deep, with covered way, pantry, a large kitchen, a smoke house, and . . . a brick stable, carriage house, etc." Edgar Snowden, who succeeded his father Samuel as editor and owner of the *Alexandria Gazette*, bought the house in 1842. It remained in the Snowden family for seventy years. In 1939 the late Hugo Black, Justice of the Supreme Court of the United States, bought the house and lived here until his death.

615. Built by Reubin (sic) Dye, who bought the northern 25 feet of the 50 foot frontage in July 1803, and the remaining 25 feet in September 1807. A wing was added on the south several years after this photograph was taken in April 1960.

Also, the central section of **609**, dating from the ownership of Joseph Harris, who pledged it in a deed of trust of 1842. Renovation of and addition to front, 1967.

605. Dates from ownership of Samuel Harper (1797–1818) or from that of John Hunter, who bought the property in 1818. (See 601.)

Also, **701,** clapboard, 2 stories, gable roof, probably mid 19th C., restored; **703,** originally clapboard, now bricktex, 2 stories, gable roof, bracket cornice, probably mid 19th C.; **705,** brick, 2 stories, gable roof, modillion cornice, probably mid 19th C.; **707, 709,** clapboard, 2 stories, gable roof, double units, probably mid 19th C.

601. In November 1797 Samuel Harper acquired a lot of ground on the southwest corner of Lee and Gibbon extending south on Lee 76 feet 7 inches and west on Gibbon 123 feet 5 inches. Tax records for 1800 show a brick house and a frame house on this lot. In April 1818 Harper sold the lot, "with the tenements and improvements," to Thomas Swayne for $3,000. A few weeks later Swayne sold it to John Hunter, the shipbuilder, for $3,800. House probably built by Harper or by Hunter.

Alexandria began as a settlement at the foot of Oronoco street attracted by a tobacco warehouse authorized by the Virginia Assembly 1730–1732. After the town was established in 1749, piers, warehouses, bake houses, taverns and dwelling houses spread south along the river. Expansion to the north and west was then blocked by Oronoco Creek. At the foot of the street Richard Conway built his "mansion house" overlooking the river. Washington dined there in 1786. As Mayor, Conway presided at the dinner Alexandrians gave General Washington on December 31, 1783, to celebrate his return after the end of the Revolutionary War.

Site of Belle Air, later Colross, was the city square bounded by Oronoco, Pendleton, Henry and Fayette streets. Built by John Potts, Jr., around 1801, it became the home of Jonathan Swift, and later of Thomson F. Mason and his family. In 1929 it was moved to Princeton, New Jersey.

609. Built by William Wilson in 1795. Twin of house at 607, each originally on half a city block. Washington dined with Mr. Wilson in 1797. Mrs. Sarah Carter was the tenant 1810–1812; Judge William Cranch in 1813. By spring of 1814 owned by John Hopkins, whose second wife was Cornelia Lee, a daughter of William Lee of Greenspring. Hopkins family lived here until after Cornelia's death in 1817. From December 1, 1817, until sometime in 1821, Mrs. Bridget Cottringer, from Philadelphia, conducted a Young Ladies' Seminary here; her portrait by Gilbert Stuart was in the Alexandria *Our Town* exhibit in 1956. John Lloyd, who married a daughter of Edmund Jennings Lee, was the tenant 1821–1823. In the autumn of 1824 Benjamin Hallowell opened his school here, and saw the Marquis de Lafayette call upon Mrs. Lee at 607. Early in 1825 Hallowell tutored young Robert E. Lee in mathematics. In 1835 purchased by Thomson F. Mason, a grandson of George Mason of Gunston Hall. In 1847 Mason's widow sold the half block to the Mount Vernon Cotton Manufacturing Company. The house and present lot were purchased in 1852 by Lucy Lyons Turner, step-daughter of Cornelia Lee Hopkins; in 1873, by Richard Bland Lee, Jr.

607. Boyhood Home of Robert E. Lee. Washington dined here with John Potts, Jr., who built the house in 1795, and with William Fitzhugh, who bought it in 1799. While surveying his lands at Four Mile Run, Washington was Fitzhugh's guest for two nights. George Washington Parke Custis, grandson of Martha Washington, came here to court a Fitzhugh daughter, Mary Lee. Fitzhugh died in 1809. By the spring of 1812 Light Horse Harry Lee and his family were living here. A year later Light Horse Harry went to the West Indies, hoping to recover from injuries received in the Baltimore riot of 1812. By the spring of 1817 his family had moved to 407 North Washington. By or before January 1818 William Henry Fitzhugh was in residence. On the 26th Mrs. Harrison Gray Otis listed among her social engagements: "Thursday, Pretty Mrs. Fitzhugh at Alexandria . . . a ball." Light Horse Harry died while journeying home in 1818. By 1821 his family were back at 607. On February 18, 1824, his son, Robert E. Lee, applied for a cadet's warrant to West Point: "I have read . . . Caesar, Sallust, Virgil, Cicero, Horace and Tacitus of the Latin authors; . . . Xenophon, Homer, Longinus of the Greek, and have studied arithmetic, algebra, and the first six books of Euclid." Lee and his family lived here until he left for West Point in June 1825. Open to the public. Admission fee.

110, 112, 114, 116, 118 North. Bolitha Laws built house at 110 in 1812. In 1835 purchased by Hannah Dick, widow of Dr. Elisha Cullen Dick, who may have lived here before moving to Botetourt County, Virginia, where she died in February 1843. Bought by James Keith Marshall in 1854. House at 112 probably dates from ownership of Isaac McLain, who bought the lot in August 1802 for an annual ground rent, and sold in September 1806 to Philip Darrell for $1,000. Purchased by Jacob Fortney in June 1811. House at 114 built by Francis Poston, who bought the lot in 1802, and pledged it, "one tenement and lot of ground," in a deed of trust in March 1815. Lot of 116 and 118 purchased by Charles Scott in 1830. In April 1832 Scott advertised "TWO BRICK HOUSES, just finished and ready for genteel families, on Patrick street between Cameron and King."

124, 126 North. Charles Bladen bought the land on which these houses stand in 1847. When the house at 126 was sold in October 1858 to Barbara Bennett, the deed referred to "the division wall of the two brick houses built by Charles Bladen."

Also, **400, 402** North, brick, 2 stories, shed roof, bracket cornice, double units, mid 19th C.; **332, 334**, clapboard re-sided, 3 stories, bracket cornice, double units, mid 19th C.; **328**, clapboard, now bricktex, 2 stories, gable roof, mid 19th C.; **324, 326**, clapboard, 2 stories, gable roof, double units, areaway, 326 with pilasters, mid 19th C.; **320**, brick, 2 stories, gable roof, modillion cornice, mid 19th C.; **316**, brick, now cast stone facade, 2 stories, gable roof, mid 19th C.; **204, 206**, flush siding and bricktex, 2 stories, gable roof, double units, mid 19th C.

115 South. Probably dates from house built by James Russell around 1812. Purchased in 1825 by the Reverend William H. Wilmer, Rector of St. Paul's Church. Sold by Wilmer's widow in August 1837. By 1850 owner was C. C. Bradley, who probably restyled the early house.

112, 114 South. Built by Isaac Gibson, probably soon after he purchased the ground on which the houses stand in May 1812. In 1833 Gibson's heirs conveyed to John W. Massie.

209 South. Two-story rear ell may have been on the lot when William Veitch sold it to John Henderson in May 1840. The three-story building on the front was added by Henderson or his heirs prior to 1860. Remained in the Henderson family until 1907.

115 North. Probably built by Caroline Grigg, wife of Joseph Grigg, after she bought the lot from the Common Council of Alexandria in July 1852 for $239. Remained in the Grigg family until 1875, when it was purchased by Edward Dunn for $1,415.

Also, North, **118** through **134**, brick, 2 stories, bracket and dentil cornice, 9 units, mid 19th C.; **133**, brick, 2 stories above basement, bracket cornice, altered, mid 19th C.; **131**, brick, 2 stories above basement, bracket cornice, mid 19th C.; **129**, **127**, brick, 2 stories, bracket cornice, double units, built with 131; **125**, **121**, clapboard, 2½ stories, arched dormers, gable roof, bracket cornice, probably mid 19th C.

116 North. Built in 1815 by Craven T. Peyton, who in October 1814 bought the quarter block that includes the site of 116 from Robert Young for $700. In 1816 Peyton sold the quarter block for $10,000, the increase in price indicating that Peyton had improved the lot. It was owned by the Union Bank and the Bank of Potomac until June 1842, when Benjamin Thomas bought it for $2,300. In 1893 Thomas' heirs sold 116, with the present lot boundaries, for $1,500.

120 South. Built by John Throop, who bought the lot in 1815. Advertised for sale at public auction in December 1817 as "that handsome and well finished brick dwelling house now in the occupation of John Throop." At the auction William Veitch was the high bidder at $2,600.

125 South. Probably dates from house built by Perlinda (Verlinda) Atkinson, to whom a lot of ground that included the site of 125 was conveyed in August 1817 for $500, or from ownership of James Atkinson, who, according to a deed of July 1828, was then living in a house on this lot. In a September 1857 deed of partition of James Atkinson's estate, this house, with a larger lot of ground, was conveyed to his son James W. Atkinson, who probably enlarged and restyled the house. In 1884 sold by court order and purchased by John Ahern for $1,500.

Also, South, **219, 217,** brick, 3 stories with ell, fretted cornice, originally double units, 219 with recent major alterations.

PITT NORTH

304. May date from ownership of Alexander Perry, or of Martin Woncher. In 1801 Perry acquired a lot beginning at the northwest corner of Pitt and Queen, running 90 feet north on Pitt, for an annual ground rent of $40. In April 1807 Perry sold to Thomas Brocchus, noting in the deed that he had agreed to convey 20 of the 90 feet to Woncher for an annual ground rent of $20. In July 1807 Brocchus conveyed to Woncher for an annual rent of $20, 20 feet fronting on Pitt, beginning 70 feet north of Queen. Today 304 fronts 42 feet on Pitt, and the house seems to be on the 20 feet conveyed to Woncher.

Also, **305, 307, 309,** clapboard, 2 stories, mid 19th C., restored.

227. Built or enlarged by Ewell C. Atwell, who in July 1854 bought the lot from Henry Brengle for $500, and in November 1863 sold it to Gilbert Simpson for $1,500.

Also, **225, 223,** clapboard, 2 stories, mid 19th C., restored; **222, 224,** brick, clapboard rear, 2 stories, 19th C. row type.

221, 219, 217, 215. Among the new buildings listed in the *Alexandria Gazette* of April 1, 1854, were these "four fine frame buildings" of William Gregory.

206, 208, 210, 212. Probably built by Moses Hepburn after June 1, 1850, when he acquired the land, in two purchases, for a total of $700. At that time there was a small frame tenement on the lot.

110. Nehemia Carson bought the northern 20 feet of the present frontage in 1810; the southern 12 feet 8 inches in 1813. When sold in 1827, pursuant to a deed of trust, the Trustees sold the two lots in one parcel for $830, because "the two lots ... were covered by one two-story brick warehouse, not susceptible of division." James Van Sant bought it in 1830. When sold in 1867, it was the "brick dwelling house ... late the residence of James Van Sant."

125. On a part of lot 112 of the town plat of 1763, conveyed to George Washington October 22, 1765. In June 1803 Washington's executors conveyed to Lawrence A. Washington that part of Lot 112 that included the sites of 123 and 125. In February 1838 Lawrence's heir sold the sites of 123 and 125 to Alexius Johnston for $275. House at 125 probably built by Johnston, who in his will dated October 29, 1842, instructed his executor to "sell my real estate which consists of a two-story frame house ... on the northwest corner of Prince and Pitt," today 125. See 123.

123. House at 125 and site of 123 purchased by William Gregory in July 1844 for $605. In 1847 Gregory sold the property to Benjamin Hughes for $750. In July 1874 Hughes conveyed to Joseph Francis Cook, for $500, the northern 30 feet 10 inches of the Pitt Street frontage "with the house on said lot and all appurtenances," today 123. Built either by Gregory or by Hughes. See 125.

229. Probably replaced the two-story brick dwelling of Colonel Charles Simms, Revolutionary officer, delegate to the Virginia Convention that ratified the Constitution of the United States, Mayor of Alexandria 1814, and a leader of the local bar. After Simms' death in 1819, purchased by his son-in-law, Cuthbert Powell. Probably built by Powell, or by the Powell heir who sold it in 1853 for $3,300.

St. Paul's Church. East side 200 block. Architect, Benjamin Latrobe. In 1809 there was one Episcopal Church in Alexandria. Its rector quarreled with some members of the Congregation and resigned. Other members sided with the Rector, and formed a new congregation. For a time meetings were held at the Independent Meeting House, then on the east side of the 200 block of South Fairfax Street. On May 2, 1817, bids for the "Carpenters' Work and Brick Work" were solicited. The corner stone was laid June 21, 1817, and the church was consecrated May 17, 1818. The building committee had problems. Latrobe was unhappy about changes made in his plans: "What a confession of ostentatious poverty! The congregation are proud enough to build a handsome front . . . but too poor to be consistent in the flanks." A dispute between the contractor and the committee was aired in the Alexandria newspaper. All ended happily. The editor of the *Alexandria Gazette* hailed the new church as "an honorable monument of the taste and liberality of the congregation."

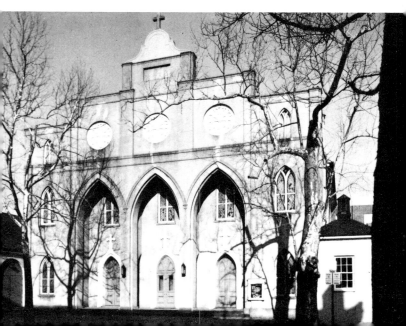

200, 202. Originally "brick warehouse or store" built by George O. Dixon and his brother John A. Dixon between 1840 and 1855, when in a deed of partition this corner lot was awarded to George. Later Victorianized.

204, 206. Built 1852–1853 by George O. Dixon and his brother James A. Dixon on land they bought in 1840.

213. Built before 1823 by Josiah H. Davis, on a lot he bought in December 1817. William Stabler purchased it in 1847.

319, 317, 315. John Keys built 319 and 317 in the spring of 1852. Contractors were John Bontz, carpenter, and James Javins, bricklayer. Recently restored. Samuel H. Devaughan purchased the lot of 315 in June 1851 for $200. Five years later he sold this "tenement and lot of ground" to William A. Cogan for $1,200. This March 1961 photograph shows restoration in progress.

208, 210. Built by George O. Dixon and his brother James A. Dixon 1852–1853. In May 1853 a Mrs. D'Laynel was living in 210.

212. Built by George O. Dixon, who purchased the lot in November 1840 for $275. In April 1852 he sold it to Captain Nathaniel Boush for $3,500.

Also, **418, 420,** clapboard, 2 stories, gable roof, originally double units, probably mid 19th C., remodeled; **421,** clapboard, 2 stories with high basement, gable roof, cast-iron posts supporting entrance porch, mid 19th C., restored; **423,** clapboard, 2 stories, gable roof, new brick rear addition, mid 19th C.; **500,** clapboard, 2 stories, gable roof, mid 19th C.

415. May date from ownership of Charles Bradford, "Mariner," who bought the lot in December 1805. In 1809 Bradford bought land adjoining on the south, beginning "at the southeast corner of the house" then owned and occupied by him.

1, 4. In April 1849 Emanuel Francis bought at public auction for $205 a lot that included the sites of these houses. Francis erected two buildings, each containing two dwelling units. In 1860 Francis sold one unit in 4 Potomac Court for $475; in 1865, one unit in 1 Potomac Court for $600. Later the two units in each building were combined, making two dwelling houses.

2. Aquila Emerson purchased the lot in June 1822, for $540, from an heir of Isaac Entwisle. The price suggests there may have been a building on the lot. Emerson sold it in May 1836 to Hugh Smith for $1,250. Emerson either built the house, or enlarged and improved an existing structure.

100 block. "Captains Row." The 1749 map of Alexandria shows that the river came to within a third of a block of present-day Lee street. By the end of the Revolutionary War, dry land had been created, through filling, to a point below Union street. Around 1784, Colonel George Gilpin, who owned the frontage on the south side, subdivided his land and began selling lots for annual ground rents. Sea captain John Harper, who owned the frontage

on the north side, followed suit. On January 18, 1827, a fire broke out on the east side of Royal street near King. Propelled by high winds, the fire raged on an erratic course that included the 100 block of Prince. A detailed account of the fire appeared in the *Alexandria Phenix Gazette* of January 23. An attempt, only partially successful, has been made to determine what buildings were on the lots before and after the fire.

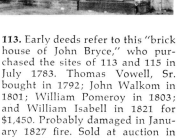

113. Early deeds refer to this "brick house of John Bryce," who purchased the sites of 113 and 115 in July 1783. Thomas Vowell, Sr. bought in 1792; John Walkom in 1801; William Pomeroy in 1803; and William Isabell in 1821 for $1,450. Probably damaged in January 1827 fire. Sold at auction in 1836 to Frederick Vaccari for $150.

111, 109. In July 1783 Captain John Harper conveyed to Michael Thorn sites of 111 and 109 for an annual ground rent. In February 1790 Thorn sold site of 111 for £75 to Thomas Vowell, Sr., who probably built the house. Thomas Vowell, Jr., and John C. Vowell bought in 1812 for $2,000. Sold in March 1827, after the January fire, to Beale Howard, for $450. Conveyed January 1831 to John Manery for $700. House at 109 probably built by Michael Thorn, who in 1794 sold to Michael O'Mara for £700. In 1815 James Robinson bought 109 for $2,150, and in 1831 John Manery purchased for $1,500. Probably both 111 and 109 renovated by Manery.

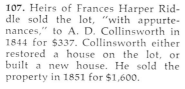

107. Heirs of Frances Harper Riddle sold the lot, "with appurtenances," to A. D. Collinsworth in 1844 for $337. Collinsworth either restored a house on the lot, or built a new house. He sold the property in 1851 for $1,600.

105, 103. Both may date from ownership of Joshua Riddle and his wife Frances, a daughter of Captain John Harper. Conveyed to Frances in 1804. When Frances' heirs sold lot of 105 to Henry Chatham in 1844 for $826, there was a brick tenement on it. Frances and others conveyed lot of 103 to John Howard in 1818 for $1,400, the price suggesting that the lot had been improved. Owned by the Howard family until 1882.

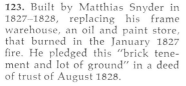

123. Built by Matthias Snyder in 1827–1828, replacing his frame warehouse, an oil and paint store, that burned in the January 1827 fire. He pledged this "brick tenement and lot of ground" in a deed of trust of August 1828.

121. Right to collect annual ground rent on this lot, and to repossess if unpaid, conveyed George Slacum in 1797. In June 1849 heirs of Dr. Frederick May, whose wife was a daughter of Slacum, conveyed this then "vacant lot" to Margaret Callender for $175. House built by Margaret Callender or by her heir after 1849.

119, 117. Both replaced frame houses destroyed in January 1827 fire. Edward McLaughlin may have built house at 119 after he purchased the lot in March 1827 for $500. Sold at auction in 1846 for $1,450. George Slacum in 1799 bought the right to collect annual ground rent on lot of 117. In October 1852 heirs of Dr. Frederick May, whose wife was a daughter of George Slacum, sold to Thomas Burns for $750. House built by Slacum heirs, or by Burns. Burns' widow sold in 1890 for $1,000.

115. Replaced a two-story brick house on the lot when it was sold in 1816 to Edward McLaughlin for $1,950. McLaughlin sold in May following the January 1827 fire as a "vacant lot of ground," for $100. Again sold for $100 in 1845. House probably built by heirs of Frederick Vaccari around 1850. Sold by court order in 1887 for $1,500.

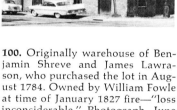

100. Originally warehouse of Benjamin Shreve and James Lawrason, who purchased the lot in August 1784. Owned by William Fowle at time of January 1827 fire—"loss inconsiderable." Photograph, June 1960. Restored and converted to residence in 1966.

106. May date from three-story brick house built by Michael Madden around 1786. In 1799 right to collect annual ground rent on this lot and the lot of 108 was conveyed to George Slacum. Purchased in 1803 by Henry Bayne of Bayne and Cartwright. Listed in account of January 1827 fire as owned by heirs of Seth Cartwright—"loss considerable." In 1830 houses at 106 and 108 sold by heirs of Warren Briscoe, whose wife was a daughter of George Slacum, to Thomas King for $450. King apparently restored 106 and 108, and sold both to John C. Vowell in 1838 for $1,000. In 1850 Vowell sold 106 for $600.

108. May date from ownership of Abel Willis (1808–1810). Owned by Jonathan C. May at time of January 1827 fire—"loss very heavy." In 1830 sold with 106 to Thomas King. John C. Vowell sold in April 1851 for $700. See 106.

114, 116, 118. House at 114 built by George Plain, who bought the lot in October 1843 for $230, and sold to Enoch Lyles for $1,600 in January 1852. Houses at 116 and 118 built by Jonathan C. May 1827–1828 to replace a "two-story segar and tobacco manufactory" and a two-story brick house lost in the January 1827 fire. In March 1829, house at 116, "a brick tenement," sold for $1,010; a month later, house at 118 for $1,282. Photograph 1964. Major alterations to 114.

127. In June 1796 Aloysius and Joseph Boone purchased the corner lot, including the site of 127, for an annual ground rent. The Boones may have built the "three-story brick warehouse owned by Mr. Norman Fitzhugh" listed in the account of the January 1827 fire, or it may have been built by Fitzhugh. Apparently some time before 1827 the property had been repossessed by heirs of Mary Harper Vowell, whose daughter was Fitzhugh's wife. Owned by the Fitzhugh family until 1867.

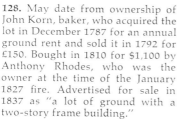

128. May date from ownership of John Korn, baker, who acquired the lot in December 1787 for an annual ground rent and sold it in 1792 for £150. Bought in 1810 for $1,100 by Anthony Rhodes, who was the owner at the time of the January 1827 fire. Advertised for sale in 1837 as "a lot of ground with a two-story frame building."

130. May date from "vendue-store" of Philip Marsteller, who acquired the lot in 1787 for an annual ground rent. Owned by the Bank of Alexandria at the time of the January 1827 fire. In the 1833 partition of the estate of Mordecai Miller, the right to collect the ground rent on this lot, conveyed to Miller in 1797, was awarded to Samuel Miller, who also bought in the property at a tax sale in March 1841. In 1877 Samuel's executors sold it, "with the buildings thereon," for $800.

200 (and 201 South Lee). Built around 1780, home of Colonel Robert Townshend Hooe, first Mayor of Alexandria (1780–1781). Washington "Dined at Colo. Hooe's" on several occasions. Hooe came from Charles County, Maryland, where during the Revolution he served on the Committee of Safety, and as Lieutenant Colonel in the 12th Maryland battalion. His partner, Richard Harrison, was a government agent in France during the Revolution, and later, United States Consul in Cadiz, Spain. The Farmers' Bank bought the property in 1811, after Hooe's death in 1809. Served as a banking house until 1910. Apparently converted to two houses some time between 1910 and 1918. 201 South Lee now being renovated and restored.

Two early frame houses formerly stood between 200 and 210. The one adjoining 200 was, 1801–1805, James Davidson's "Ships' Tavern."

210. Built 1785–1786 by Colonel Michael Swope, formerly of York, Pennsylvania. He was a member of the Pennsylvania Committee of Safety in 1775, and was serving in the Pennsylvania line when captured at Fort Washington, New York, in November 1776. On March 6, 1778, the British sent word that they were "willing that Colonel Swope be returned for Governor Franklin." William Franklin, son of Benjamin Franklin, was the loyalist governor of New Jersey. His arrest had been ordered by the Provincial Congress of New Jersey in June 1776. Jacob, a son of Michael, was the first mayor of Staunton, Virginia, under its 1801 charter.

212, 214. "Double dwelling house," built by William Hartshorne around 1787. Mordecai Miller, first a silversmith, later a prosperous merchant, bought the property in 1794, and for a few years lived in one of the houses. In 1802 his tenant was Dr. William Daingerfield. In 1811 an anonymous letter in an Alexandria newspaper complained of the danger of fire from the use of one of the houses as a bakery. An heir of Miller sold in 1839 to James Green.

216. Built by Charles Slade between 1805 and 1815. Replaced an earlier frame house owned by Philip Wanton.

201. Athenaeum. Originally the Old Dominion Bank, built 1851–1852: "The carpenter's work by B. H. Jenkins, E. Francis, bricklayer." Replaced a large frame warehouse. Now headquarters and gallery of the Northern Virginia Fine Arts Association. Open to the public.

207. Colonel William Fairfax of Belvoir bought the quarter block on which this house stands at the first sale of town lots in July 1749. His son and heir, George William Fairfax, sold it before he went to England in 1771. In June 1790 William Hodgson purchased from Captain John Harper the part of the lot on which the house stands for £1,650. In May 1799 he married Portia Lee, a daughter of William Lee of Greenspring. Hodgson and his family moved in 1803 to "Bellevue," north of the town. Tax records for 1810 list John Hopkins, whose wife was Portia's sister Cornelia, as the occupant.

215. John Harper conveyed the site to Aaron Hewes in November 1783. A 1796 insurance policy covered a two-story brick building with a "Hatter's Shop built of wood" on the front. The shop was removed and the brick house extended to Prince, with a story added, before 1829, when Hewes' heirs conveyed it to Hewes' widow for her lifetime.

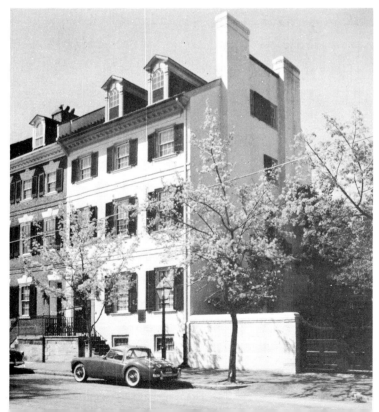

213, 211, 209. Built by Captain John Harper. With 215 and 207, the finest 18th century street facade in Alexandria. House at 213 on the lot when Harper conveyed it in April 1793 in trust for his daughter Peggy. Tax records for 1810 list Alexander Moore as the occupant; for 1811–1812, William Wilson. Peggy's husband, John C. Vowell, survived her, and in 1844 conveyed it to their daughter Eliza Douglass, wife of John Douglass. House at 211 completed in the summer of 1793. By 1802, perhaps earlier, Dr. Elisha Cullen Dick was the tenant. He may have lived there until he moved "to the country" in 1820. House at 209 built around 1786. Dr. James Craik was the tenant 1789–1790, and perhaps until he moved to 210 Duke in 1796. Traditionally the home of Dr. Dick. It is possible he lived in the house at 209 as well as the house at 211, because early records do not cover every year. All evidence now available places him in 211. Both Dr. Craik and Dr. Dick attended Washington in his last illness.

House at 217 may date from ownership of Harper heirs who in 1813 sold the corner lot, the site of 217 and of 219, to Matthew Robinson. In 1830 William Robinson, son of Matthew, was living in a "two-story frame tenement" on this lot. An 1835 deed indicates there was a brick building on the corner, which, restyled, may today be house at 219. Owned by Thomas Burns and his heirs from 1835 to 1901, when it was sold to the Mercantile Building and Loan Association for $2,300. Converted to a residence after 1912.

305. Early insurance policies show George Slacum's two-story frame house here in 1796; George Slacum's two-story brick house in 1805; and by 1823, a three-story brick house owned by Slacum's heirs.

Also, **302**, brick, 3 stories, "executed" for Harrison Jacobs, 1852; **304**, clapboard, 2 stories with areaway, early-mid 19th C.; **306**, brick, 2 stories, false front, good proportions indicate an early building; **309**, brick, 2½ stories, built between 1805 and 1815; **310**, brick, 3 stories, false front, office of *Alexandria Gazette* when burned 1862, rebuilt c. 1864 incorporating old east and south walls; **311**, clapboard, 2½ stories, may date from house on lot when John Wise sold to Jacob Resler in 1796, restored 1967; **314**, brick, 3 stories, on lot in 1830, probably rebuilt after 1862 fire at 310.

415, 413. Originally the Bank of Potomac, built 1804–1807. When renovated 1958–1960 five keys were found, all five to be inserted to enter the vault. Headquarters of the Restored Government of Virginia 1863–1865.

Also, **411,** brick, 3 stories, mid 19th C.

405, 403, 401. Traditionally, house at 405, with late brick facade, dates from ownership of William Sewell, "peruke maker," among whose customers was George Washington. Sewell acquired the quarter block on which the house stands in 1754 for an annual ground rent. House at 401 probably built by Samuel Miller, who bought the lot in 1858. It replaced a large frame building on the site in 1814. Alley house at 403 built before 1883, when Samuel H. Janney, then the owner, bequeathed to his son Henry the rents accruing from "the three-story brick house and the small two-story brick house adjoining thereto on the northwest corner of Prince and Royal."

400, 402, 404. Probably date from 1797–1798. In March 1797 George McMunn and Jonathan Pancoast entered into an agreement permitting Pancoast to extend the walls of a brick house he was about to build on the site of 402 onto McMunn's land on the east and on the west, and permitting McMunn to attach buildings to Pancoast's walls. Alexander McKenzie bought 400 in 1814. John Horner purchased 402 in 1800, and 404 in 1801. Photograph April 1959.

412, 414. Listed under "Local Items" in the *Alexandria Gazette* of March 6, 1852: "The contractors for the carpenters' work of the beautiful new three story dwelling houses on Prince Street belonging to William N. McVeigh, which have just been finished, ... were George and William Davis, who turn out as handsome specimens of work in their line as can be shown anywhere."

513. There was a brick tenement on the lot when John Graham, a Scottish sea captain, bought it in December 1843 for $1,750. Around 1855 (see 511) Captain Graham either enlarged and restyled, or replaced, the early house. According to family tradition, Captain Graham sailed from Great Britain to Alexandria for some years before he brought his family here. His daughter Mamie lived in the house until she died at 93.

511. Built by Isaac Buckingham around 1855 when he and John C. Graham, then the owner of the lot of 513, divided an eleven foot alley running north from Prince between their properties.

517. Built around 1775 by Patrick Murray, who acquired the quarter block on which it stands December 20, 1774, for an annual ground rent. In 1792 Murray advertised on this site "a commodious framed house, with four rooms and three fireplaces on the first floor . . . two rooms on the second, and a kitchen annexed." Owned by one family since John Douglas Brown purchased it in 1816, it is perhaps the least altered of the surviving early buildings of Alexandria.

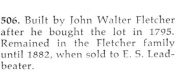

506. Built by John Walter Fletcher after he bought the lot in 1795. Remained in the Fletcher family until 1882, when sold to E. S. Leadbeater.

Also, **504**, brick, 2½ stories, early 19th C., Victorianized; **507**, brick, 3 stories, built 1854 by widow of Richard Marshall Scott, replacing early frame house of Ezra Lunt; **508**, brick, 3 stories, mid 19th C.; **512**, brick, 2½ stories, false front, good proportions indicate an early building.

520. Originally included house at 202 South St. Asaph. Built before 1796 by John Korn and Jacob Wisemiller, biscuit bakers. Purchased in December 1832 by Horatio Clagett, who announced that he had "lately removed from the City Hotel and . . . established a Boarding House at the corner of Prince and St. Asaph street. . . . Dinner parties will be furnished whenever required and Hacks furnished Gentlemen and Ladies who wish to visit Mount Vernon and return to dinner."

607, 605. Probably built or restyled
by William B. Klipstein, who in
1858 bought 607 for $3,000 from
William H. McKnight, who had
purchased it from his brother
Charles in 1852 for $1,150. Klip-
stein acquired the lot of 605 in
1853 by assuming payment of an
annual ground rent of $60.

706. Thomas Swann, a prominent attorney, lived on this corner from around 1803 to 1825, in a two-story brick house 42 feet long and 32 feet wide; on the east, a two-story brick wing, 31 feet long and 20 feet wide. In 1832 Swann, then living in Washington, D. C., sold to Henry Daingerfield, who probably restyled the house in the Victorian manner. In October 1905 the Sisters of the Holy Cross, who had recently bought the property, announced they would build an annex on Columbus, three stories and an attic, 63 feet long and 34 feet wide, to enlarge the building for the use of St. Mary's Academy. Until recently, Carter Hall, nurses home.

711. May date from dwelling house of James Patton, who bought the quarter block on which it stands in 1797. Purchased in 1811 for $6,550 by William Fowle, who enlarged and restyled the house. Family tradition credits the facade to Charles Bulfinch. By 1842 the grounds included the north side of the 700 block, and extended north 140 feet on Washington and north on Columbus to within 100 feet of King. Fowle served as the president of the Alexandria Canal Company, and as president of the Old Dominion Bank. He died in 1860, in his 77th year.

804. John Marshall may have visited here when traveling to and from Washington, D. C., during the years he served as Chief Justice of the United States. Marshall's cousin, James Keith, Jr., built the house around 1815–1820.

806. Built by the Reverend James T. Johnston on the lot he bought in 1850. Johnston was rector of St. Paul's Church from October 1833 to February 1859. Owned by the United Daughters of the Confederacy. Not open to the public.

804, 806, 808, 810, 812, 814. In 1854 Lawrence B. Taylor bought the house at 808, built by Thomas Jacobs around 1817. In 1858 Taylor pledged it as security for $1,700 he owed to John A. Washington of Mount Vernon. Taylor served as mayor of Alexandria 1850–1853, and in the Virginia Assembly. Lots of 810 and 812 were purchased by George D. Fowle in 1851 for a total of $247. In 1868 both lots sold for $1,175. Probably Fowle built the house at 810, and the house at 812 was built by the 1868 purchaser, William F. Vincent. In 1912 the house at 812 sold for $5,000. House at 814, restyled, may date from a house on the lot when sold at auction in 1835 to Leonard Cooke for $72, and an annual ground rent of $20.83.

811. In 1855 William H. Fowle, son of William Fowle of 711 Prince, paid William Bayne $18,000 for this house and garden. Bayne bought the land in 1849 for a total of $850. In 1856, when Fowle conveyed it in trust for his wife Eliza, a daughter of James H. Hooe, it was the "ground on which said William H. Fowle now resides."

"A BLACK NEWFOUNDLAND DOG, of moderate size, long curling hair, feet and tip of tail white, answers to the name 'Kennear,' has been missing for a day or two. A liberal reward will be given for any information which will lead to his discovery. WILLIAM H. FOWLE." *Alexandria Gazette,* November 19, 1847.

819, 817. Built by Leonard and Thomas Cooke around 1803. On May 5 of that year Leonard conveyed to Thomas a half interest in two lots that he had purchased from Francis Peyton, one on June 23, 1796, the other on May 3, 1803. Together the lots provided the 42 foot frontage of the two houses on Prince. In October 1807 the Cookes divided some properties they owned jointly, including these two brick dwelling houses. Leonard was given 819; Thomas, 817.

Also, **803**, brick, 3 stories, gable roof, built by John McCobb c. 1814; **818**, brick, 3 stories, gable roof, bracket cornice, mid-late 19th C.

Also, **905**, brick, 3 stories, gable roof, sawtooth cornice, early 19th C.; **916**, brick, 3 stories, built c. 1812 by Benjamin Baden; **919**, brick, 3 stories, molded brick cornice, early-mid 19th century.

1010, 1012. House at 1010 built either by Benjamin Baden, who bought the lot from William Wright in 1806, or by William Veitch, to whom Baden sold in May 1817. When Veitch conveyed to John McIver for $3,180 in April 1818, he reserved the right to build on the west gable end. Therefore house at 1012 built by Veitch between April 1818 and September 1824, when Veitch sold to John Harper for $3,000.

1016. Probably built by Reuben Bowie to whom Alexander Perry conveyed the lot in March 1818 for $230 and an annual ground rent of $25. Bowie sold to Matthias Snyder in May 1822 for $1,000 and assuming payment of the ground rent. When Snyder pledged it in a deed of trust in May 1847, Bernard Hooe was the tenant.

1020. Probably built by Richard Stanton. His father-in-law, Alexander Perry, conveyed the corner lot to him in 1823 for $5 and an annual ground rent of $50. In 1830 Stanton pledged the house in a deed of trust.

Also, **1004**, brick, stone trim, 2 stories when built by James Campbell c. 1807, probably enlarged and restyled by James Dyson, who bought in 1868; **1014**, brick, 3 stories, originally 2 stories, wood lintels with corner blocks, early 19th C.

1113. Lot owned by James Harris when built 1816–1818 with 1115 and 1117. Owned by George W. Carlin 1835–1837; sold to Benedict C. Milburn, potter, in 1838; occupied by William C. Reynolds in late 1830's.

1117. Lot owned by James McGuire when built, with 1113 and 1115, as three units in 1816–1818.

Also, **1124**, clapboard, 2 stories, dentil cornice, probably early 19th C.

1111, 1109, 1107. Built around 1804–1806: 1111 by John Lightfoot; 1109 by Edward Dailey; and 1107 by Frederick May.

1105, 1103, 1101. Built by Leonard and Thomas Cooke around 1804–1806.

1112, 1114. With 1108 and 1110, four units built by Alexander Veitch around 1818.

Also, **1201**, brick, 2 stories, gable roof, brick modillion cornice, early 19th C.; **1208**, **1210**, double units, brick, 2 stories, low pitched roof, remodeled, probably mid 19th C.

139

310. Originally clapboard, now bricktex, this house is on a quarter block owned by Thomas Longden, who was killed in 1755, when serving under General Braddock. There was a "tenement" on this site when Longden's heirs divided his estate in 1816.

From 1774, perhaps earlier, to 1787, the tavern of John Lomax on the south side of Princess between Lee and Fairfax was the center of the social life of the town. Dancing assemblies were held. Members of the early Masonic Lodge dined there, as did General Washington and the Chevalier LaLuzerne, with a "number of gentlemen." The Sons of St. Patrick entertained at "elegant Balls" on St. Patrick's Day and the "Anniversary of Tamminy." On November 15, 1784, "Gentlemen of this State and Maryland convened" to organize the Potomac Company. For several years the Company met here to transact business, with General Washington presiding. Lomax died in 1787, and Henry McCue took over the tavern. By this time Alexandria had more elegant establishments, and McCue was left with a waterfront clientele. On April 25, 1790, Arthur Lee wrote from Alexandria: "I am agreeably situated here on a Bank commanding the Harbour, which is now pretty well filled with shipping." From 1790 to 1791 Lee lived in a frame dwelling house, "with a clever garden," on the northeast corner of Princess and Lee.

711. Dates from house built 1797–1799 by John F. Smith, on a lot purchased from the Reverend David Griffith. Bought in 1853 by Captain William J. Boothe, who went to sea in his youth, and later became a leader in the business community. Between 1865 and 1870 Boothe doubled the size of the house. In 1913–1914 Mr. and Mrs. Gardner L. Boothe restored the house, moving the western front a foot or two forward to align it with the eastern front, which included the door. The porches were added at that time. Now the law offices of the firm headed by Armistead Boothe.

Also **604**, **606**. Brick, 2 stories, false front, nucleus probably early 19th C.

QUEEN

325, 323, 321, 319. Built 1818 by Presley Barker and James McGuire.

Also, **408, 410,** clapboard, 2 stories, mid 19th C. row type; **422,** originally clapboard, 2 stories, probably mid 19th C.; **424,** clapboard, 2 stories, probably early 19th C.; **415, 419, 423, 425, 427,** clapboard, 2 stories and **421,** brick, 2 stories, contemporary with 413-403.

317. Probably built by Mary Dudley, who bought the lot with a frame house on it in 1850 for $150, and sold in 1858 for $920. A 1796 insurance policy shows Robert Lyle's "two-story wooden dwelling house" on this site.

308. In August 1868 Benjamin F. Young bought the lot of 308 for $600. He sold the property in 1876 for $3,000. The substantial increase in price suggests Young built this house.

312. Built by William Summers in 1798. Advertised as having "with the back building, ... ten good rooms, neatly finished, and a large dry cellar." Richard Marshall Scott of "Bush Hill" bought it in November 1816. Scott was president of the Farmers' Bank of Alexandria.

307, 305. Built around 1860 by William Chatham, who, with James Chatham, bought at auction in October 1859 the lots on which 307, 305, 303 and 301 stand. These four houses are examples of early compatible construction, neatly balancing the four 1818 houses on the northeast corner of Queen and Royal.

303, 301. Built around 1860 by James Chatham. The early Long Ordinary was on this quarter block. On April 3, 1755, the proprietor, Nathaniel Smith, announced that he was "going out as a Sutler" to Braddock's camp, and was selling his establishment, "suitable for a tavern, 82 feet long, with a kitchen, meat house and stable." The ordinary was destroyed by fire in November 1800.

413, 411, 409, 407, 405, 403 and **302** North Royal. In June 1838 Joseph Janney bought the half block on the north side of the 400 block of Queen. Janney, and later the executors of his estate, subdivided and sold lots 1859–1872. In the spring of 1871 the *Alexandria Gazette* noted the improvement of this half block, "which from being an . . . unsightly looking cavity, has been made level with the street, and almost filled with buildings."

418. May date from mid 19th century. The site is a part of a larger lot conveyed by James Green to Henry Brengle in 1854. Not sold with present lot boundaries until bought in 1881 by William Smith, who probably remodeled the house.

525, 523. House at 525 built by John Hollensbury soon after he bought the lot in 1801 for $200. Alley house at 523 probably built by his daughter Julia Hollensbury, who died in 1901. Recently bricks have been found in the sidewalk on the west side of the 400 block of South Washington street with "Hollensbury, Alex., D. C." impressed on the under sides.

511. May date from house of Andrew Judge mentioned in a 1784 deed conveying land on the east. Enlarged and altered.

504, 506. Double units, built around 1853. House at 504 by William Arnold, at 506 by Alexander Arnold.

508. May date from ownership of Thomas Preston (1809–1830). Preston sold to Samuel Bartle in 1830.

509, 507. May date from ownership of Samuel Bartle, or earlier. In 1834 Bartle purchased the right to collect annual ground rent on the quarter block that includes houses at 501 through 511. In 1872 William H. Bartle purchased 501 through 507 from other Bartle heirs. House at 509 was awarded Rudolph Bartle in the 1872 division of Samuel's estate.

Also, **514, 516,** clapboard, 2 stories, and **518,** clapboard, 2 stories, may have been on the land when sold by Hannah Wilson in July 1851; **513, 515,** clapboard flounder, 2 stories with leanto, late 18th-early 19th C.; **517,** brick, 3 stories, sawtooth cornice, early 19th C.; **519,** clapboard, 2 stories, late 18th C.; **524,** brick, 3 stories, 19th C.; **526,** brick, 3 stories, molded cornice, 19th C.

510. Probably built by Samuel Bartle after he bought the lots of 510 and 508 from Thomas Preston in 1830.

611, 609, 607. In June 1807 William Veitch bought the site of 611 for $250. When Veitch sold to John C. Vowell in 1815 for $4,000, Camillus Griffith was living in the house. Andrew Schofield built the house at 609 around 1810. House at 607, contemporary of 609, restyled, also built by Schofield.

603. Built by Robert L. Brockett around 1853 as an addition to his Alexandria Academy at 601. Both 601 and 603 advertised in February 1858 as "the ALEXANDRIA ACADEMY ... buildings of brick, three stories ... fully supplied with gas and water, and ... heated by flues. ... built expressly for an extensive Boarding School ... but admit of change into three dwellings." House at 603 sold October 1865 for $6,000.

601. With house at 603, Robert L. Brockett's Alexandria Academy. Brockett bought a lot that included the site of 601 in February 1842. House built before 1850. Conveyed in February 1868 for $1,500.

Alexandria library lot, north side 700 block, was the site of the Quaker burying ground, conveyed May 8, 1785, by Thomas West to the Society of Friends. Dr. Elisha Cullen Dick is buried there.

Also, **812, 814,** brick, 2 stories, gable roof, double units, probably mid 19th C.; **824, 826,** clapboard, now bricktex, 2 stories, originally with common gable roof, bracket cornice and chimney, 824 Victorianized, 826 remodeled 1970, mid 19th C.

Also, **904, 906,** brick, 2 stories, gable roof, sawtooth cornice, double units, mid 19th C.; **908, 910, 912,** 2 stories, re-sided with metal, triple units, mid 19th C.

Also, **1007, 1009,** clapboard, now bricktex, 2 stories above basement, double units, mid 19th C.; **1024,** clapboard, 2 stories, gable roof, early-mid 19th C.

The early powder house was on the southwest corner of Queen and Fayette. On July 20, 1793, Charles Alexander conveyed the site to the Mayor and Commonality of Alexandria, for twenty years, one ear of Indian corn to be paid on the last day of December each year, "if same be lawfully demanded."

207. May have been on the lot when Charles Simms sold in July 1799 to James Kennedy, Jr. The price is left blank in the deed. In December 1805 Kennedy conveyed it to Hugh Smith for $500. In 1856 a son of Smith pledged in a deed of trust "that lot of ground covered by the brick warehouse on the north side of Fayette [Ramsay] Alley." For a time workshop of the Little Theater of Alexandria. Remodeled 1964. Now a shop below, living quarters above.

149

202, 204, 206. During renovation of the house at 204 a new 1874 penny was found in the old plaster, indicating that these houses were built in that year by John and George Harlow, who owned the lots. An early bath house was on the rear of the lots of 204 and 206. In May 1813 the proprietor announced that two separate baths were kept exclusively for ladies.

208. In May 1799 John Duff offered to sell this new three-story brick house, and in 1801 sold to Robert Patton for £1,000. Some tenants of Patton were: Walter Jones, son-in-law of Charles Lee (1802); Dr. Henry Rose (1805); and Ferdinando Fairfax, third son of Bryan, Eighth Lord Fairfax (1814). Ferdinando was remembered as "a man of highly cultivated mind" who dispensed lavish hospitality. Perhaps too lavish. In October 1815 a United States Marshal advertised a sale of Fairfax's household goods at his "late residence on Royal" to satisfy a judgment against him. In April 1816 Patton sold to Oliver P. Finley for $6,000.

220. Built around 1854 by Joseph McLean, who bought the lot in November 1853 for $300. Sold to David Appich in July 1865 for $3,700.

207. Probably on the lot when Patrick Allison sold to Jacob Fortney in 1793 for £450. Fortney's son and namesake left to his widow Rosina all the "land whereon are my stable, dwelling house and blacksmith's shop, it being late the property of my father." His widow married George H. Duffey. Her descendants say that she nursed the "Female Stranger" who died at Gadsby's Hotel in October 1816.

221, 219, 217. These three houses built by James McGuire, "House Joiner." He bought the lot of 221 for $500 in October 1832. Sold for $1,175 in 1852. House at 219 built between 1811, when McGuire purchased the lot for $666, and 1814, when tax records show Noblett Herbert, son of Thomas Herbert, the tenant. On November 18, 1813, Noblett married Mary Lee Washington, niece of Bushrod Washington, at Mount Vernon. McGuire lived at 217, built around 1796, until he died of "Dropsy" in his 76th year. House restyled either by J. Newton Harper, who bought it in 1853, or by James McCullough, to whom Harper sold in 1858.

Coffee House and City Hotel.
Southwest corner Royal and Cameron. Traditionally, the Coffee House is on the site of, and may incorporate, Charles Mason's 1752 ordinary or inn. Washington's accounts show payments for lodgings and meals at Mason's in 1755, 1756, 1757 and 1760. After the death of Mason's widow in 1761, the executors of her estate, John Carlyle and John Dalton, managed the property. A tenant was a Mrs. Hawkins, and Washington's accounts list payments to her in 1774 and 1775. After Dalton's death in 1777, the land on which the two buildings stand was sold to Edward Owens, who in January 1782 conveyed it to John Wise. Wise probably enlarged and restyled, or replaced, Mason's early building. In November 1785 it was announced that dancing assemblies for the coming season would be held in "Mr. Wise's new Room." By the spring of 1788 Wise was keeping tavern in Thomas Herbert's build-

ing on the northeast corner of Fairfax and Cameron. He remained there until after his City Hotel was completed in 1792. Wise leased the City Hotel to John Gadsby from October 1796 until December 1802, when the lease was renewed, with the Coffee House added. Under Gadsby's management, 1796–1808, the City Hotel became famous for the luxury of its accommodations. Here were held assemblies, Washington birthnight balls, and testimonial dinners.

In addition to Washington, distinguished guests included John Adams, Thomas Jefferson, James Madison, James Monroe, John Quincy Adams, and the Marquis de Lafayette. The local gentry came here to enjoy performances of traveling musicians and players, and to attend meetings of the St. Andrew's Society, the Alexandria Library Company, and the local Golf Club. When the American wing of the Metropolitan Museum opened in 1924, it displayed the re-

constructed ball room of the City Hotel. The original woodwork was purchased by the Museum in 1917. In 1929 American Legion Post No. 24 purchased the two buildings. Many groups aided in maintaining them, including the Virginia and Alexandria chapters of the Daughters of the American Revolution, the Alexandria Committee of the Colonial Dames of America, the Garden Club of Alexandria, the Children of the American Revolution, and the Alexandria Association. In 1949 the late Colonel Charles Beatty Moore and his wife, historian Gay Montague Moore, purchased the original doorway from the Metropolitan Museum. It was reinstalled on November 11, 1949. The two buildings are now owned, and being restored, by the city. Architect, J. Everette Fauber, Jr. Admission fee.

FOR THE BIRTH NIGHT BALL
The Subscriber desirous of aiding the Ladies of Alexandria in the best display of their charms . . . has on hand for their accommodation CORSETTS, newly improved and approved by a Lady whose judgment of delicate dress is inferior to none.

Also, **302**, clapboard, 3 stories, brick addition, early 19th C.; **224, 222** and **214**, brick, 3 stories, mid-late 19th C.; **209**, originally engine house of Hydraulion Fire Company, built 1856, then "surmounted by a handsome steeple 32 feet high."

William Ramsay's George Tavern, a frame building, stood on the northwest corner of Royal and Cameron until it was demolished in February 1870. When advertised for rent in 1760, it contained "Three Fire-Places below Stairs, a very good Bar, and six Rooms above; a Kitchen adjoining . . . a Dining Room 24 feet by 18 feet, a Room of the same Dimensions above it, in which there is a very good London BILLIARD TABLE." It was replaced by the present three-story brick building, now owned by the city.

119, 115. May, enlarged and restyled, date from earlier buildings on the lots acquired in two purchases by Benjamin Barton in 1864 and 1866 for a total of $2,825. Barton and his father were early Alexandria silversmiths and clockmakers.

112. The funeral accounts of George Washington list $88 paid Joseph and Henry Ingle for a mahogany coffin, with "silver plate engraved, furnished with lace." In May 1795 Joseph Ingle acquired 112 for an annual ground rent of $50. In June he announced that he continued to carry on the "Cabinet and Chair-Making Business" at his shop on Royal. Ingle sold in 1817 for $1,500, the buyer to assume payment of the annual ground rent, suggesting that Ingle improved it.

217, 215. Probably built by Edmund Jennings Lee on a part of a quarter block his wife Sarah Lee inherited from her uncle, Arthur Lee. On October 1, 1817, the Lees conveyed to Samuel Carson for $2,500, the lots of 219, 217 and 215, with two brick houses and a "south shed."

213. Probably built by Thomas Davy around 1834. When Davy bought the lot in December 1833 it contained the wooden warehouse of Ephraim Evans, an earlier owner. In his will, recorded January 2, 1877, Davy bequeathed the "House and lot on Royal street which I have occupied as a Dwelling" to his adopted daughter Margaret, the wife of A. C. Harmon.

122. A 1796 insurance policy shows that Henry Walker was living here in a dwelling house of wood, two stories high, 22 feet by 18 feet, valued at $1,000. By 1815 Alexander Baggett was the owner, and his tenant was Samuel Baggett.

Also, **114**, brick, 2 stories, and **116, 118**, brick, 3 stories, mid 19th C.; **120**, originally clapboard, new brick facade, 2 stories, probably 18th C.; **130**, brick, 2 stories, commercial building on corner, 19th C., later additions.

214, 216, 218. Built by Reuben Johnston who bought the land on which these three houses stand in 1815 for $1,031. In 1844 Johnston heirs sold 214 and 216 to John T. Evans for $2,400.

220. A deed of May 1, 1828, conveying to Edward McLaughlin, for $245, twenty feet of the present frontage on Royal, mentions a frame workshop on the lot. In April 1829 McLaughlin purchased three feet adjoining on the north. In 1832 he conveyed this house, and another on the northeast corner of Cameron and Royal, in a deed of gift to his daughter Bridget, reserving the right to live, during his natural life, in "all or either of the aforesaid tenements."

317. Sarah Thomas sold A. D. Collinsworth the lots of 317, 315, 313 and 311 in May 1847 for $400. Collinsworth was living in the house at 317 in 1850.

316. Originally the parsonage, now the office, of the Presbyterian Meeting House. In July 1787 Robert Brockett agreed to "prepare a house of certain dimensions" for £268.

305, 303. Rear wing of house at 404 Duke, built 1808. May incorporate a brick smoke house of Dr. Elisha Cullen Dick shown on the plat of a 1796 insurance policy.

St. Mary's Roman Catholic Church.
East side 300 block. The first
church, built 1789–1793, serving
the Roman Catholic community,
was on the southeast corner of
Washington and Church streets.
The adjoining cemetery survives.
On St. Patrick's Day in 1788 Washington dined with Colonel John
Fitzgerald. Traditionally, the building of the church was discussed,
and Washington contributed to the
building fund. In May 1789 Dennis
Foley forbade "any person whatever . . . to take away any of the
building materials of the Roman
Catholic Church." A July 11, 1793,
notice of the celebration of July 14,
French independence day, included
an oration to be delivered by Citizen D. F. Donnant at the Roman
Church. In 1809 the Reverend
Francis Neale of Georgetown purchased the Methodist Meeting
House on Chapel Alley. The alley
runs south from Duke midway between Fairfax and Royal. Today
part of the church is on the meeting house lot. By 1817 Father Neale
had purchased additional land. On

March 4, 1827, a new church was
consecrated. The evolution of the
church has been reported over the
years in the *Alexandria Gazette*.

Also, **315**, **313**, **311**, clapboard, 2
stories, gable roof, triple units, renovated or built by A. D. Collinsworth
c. 1847.

Also, **406**, **408**, brick, 2 stories, gable
roof, areaway, double units, mid 19th
C.; **414**, clapboard, 2 stories, now
stucco ends, probably mid 19th C.;
415, originally clapboard, now asbestos,
2½ stories, gable roof with dormer,
probably early 19th C.; **424**, brick, 2
stories, gable roof, probably early 19th
C., Victorian detail, remodeled 1960.

157

429, 427. Built by James H. Wilkinson to whom the heirs of Sarah Griffith, daughter of the Reverend David Griffith, sold the lots in 1868 for a total of $400. In December 1894, 429 sold at public auction to John S. Beach for $1,800. In August 1883, 427 sold to James Duncan for $920.

Also, **333, 331,** clapboard, 2 stories, probably early 19th C., 333 restored; **327, 325,** frame, 2 stories, mid 19th C., restored; **323, 319,** clapboard, 2 stories, mid 19th C.; **315,** clapboard, 2 stories, gable roof, early 19th C., remodeled 1970; **313,** clapboard, 2 stories, mid 19th C., restored; **309, 307,** clapboard, 2 stories over basement, mid 19th C. restored.

403. City Jail. An Act of Congress of March 2, 1831, provided for a payment to the architect Charles Bulfinch, "for extra services in planning and superintending the building of . . . the jail in Alexandria." The central section, with gable roof, may be the original structure. Enlarged from time to time.

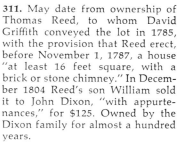

311. May date from ownership of Thomas Reed, to whom David Griffith conveyed the lot in 1785, with the provision that Reed erect, before November 1, 1787, a house "at least 16 feet square, with a brick or stone chimney." In December 1804 Reed's son William sold it to John Dixon, "with appurtenances," for $125. Owned by the Dixon family for almost a hundred years.

219. Built by Burrill T. Plummer on a lot he purchased in May 1853. His "dwelling house" when he pledged it in 1857 as security in a deed of trust.

Also, **217**, permastone veneer, 2 stories, probably 19th C.

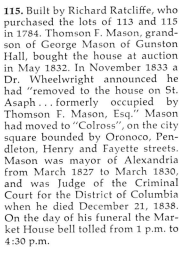

115. Built by Richard Ratcliffe, who purchased the lots of 113 and 115 in 1784. Thomson F. Mason, grandson of George Mason of Gunston Hall, bought the house at auction in May 1832. In November 1833 a Dr. Wheelwright announced he had "removed to the house on St. Asaph . . . formerly occupied by Thomson F. Mason, Esq." Mason had moved to "Colross", on the city square bounded by Oronoco, Pendleton, Henry and Fayette streets. Mason was mayor of Alexandria from March 1827 to March 1830, and was Judge of the Criminal Court for the District of Columbia when he died December 21, 1838. On the day of his funeral the Market House bell tolled from 1 p.m. to 4:30 p.m.

113. May date from around 1785. Tax records for 1787 show that the owner, Richard Ratcliffe, had tenants in both 115 and 113. In 1808 Ratcliffe sold 113 to Edmund Jennings Lee, uncle of Robert E. Lee. Abraham Faw purchased it in 1811.

Also, **121,** brick, 3 stories over basement, built by Burrill T. Plummer c. 1852.

208. In July 1870 William H. Mc-Knight pledged in a deed of trust this lot on which he was "engaged in building a brick dwelling house." A deed of June 1854 described it as containing a frame tenement occupied by McKnight. An heir, William Presley McKnight, in his will recorded in November 1927, bequeathed the house to Elizabeth F. Jones, for her lifetime, and after her death, to the Second Presbyterian Church, "for the Manse of that Church." William H. McKnight was the grandson of William McKnight, who owned one of the town's early taverns, on the northwest corner of King and Royal. The father of William H. was the sea captain John McKnight, who was captured by the French near the Capes of Virginia in 1797, and again in 1798 near Cadiz. John's brother Charles commanded the Independent Blues of Alexandria at the 1814 battle of the White House on the Potomac.

212. Built by William H. McKnight who bought the lot at public auction in April 1855. On November 4, 1856, McKnight conveyed the lot, "improved by a three-story brick dwelling house," to D. Boyd Smith for $8,500. On the same day Smith bought the southern 22 feet of the present lot. The elaborate molding over the doorway has been removed.

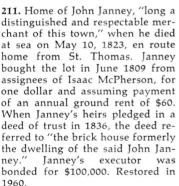

211. Home of John Janney, "long a distinguished and respectable merchant of this town," when he died at sea on May 10, 1823, en route home from St. Thomas. Janney bought the lot in June 1809 from assignees of Isaac McPherson, for one dollar and assuming payment of an annual ground rent of $60. When Janney's heirs pledged in a deed of trust in 1836, the deed referred to "the brick house formerly the dwelling of the said John Janney." Janney's executor was bonded for $100,000. Restored in 1960.

Also, **202.** See 520 Prince.

209. When William McVeigh bought the lot in 1851 there was a frame tenement on it. McVeigh purchased the brick house at 211 in 1847. He replaced the frame house at 209 with the present brick house, and restyled 211 to match 209. During the 1861–1865 occupation of Alexandria by Federal troops, 209 was the residence of the military governor.

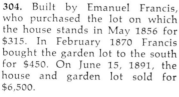

304. Built by Emanuel Francis, who purchased the lot on which the house stands in May 1856 for $315. In February 1870 Francis bought the garden lot to the south for $450. On June 15, 1891, the house and garden lot sold for $6,500.

Also, **302**, clapboard, 3 stories, brick ell, probably early 19th C., restyled; **312**, clapboard, 3 stories, probably early 19th C., Victorianized; **314**, clapboard, 3 stories, probably early 19th C., Greek Revival.

308, 310. Double houses built by Emanuel Francis, who purchased the lot in February 1864 for $350. Sold under a deed of trust in March, 1893, for $2,260.

The first Quaker Meeting House was on the lot of 311, which was conveyed to Trustees of the Society of Friends in April 1785 by Benjamin Shreve. In May 1841 succeeding Trustees sold to William Stabler for $189.

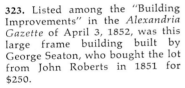

323. Listed among the "Building Improvements" in the *Alexandria Gazette* of April 3, 1852, was this large frame building built by George Seaton, who bought the lot from John Roberts in 1851 for $250.

321. This flounder house, like the flounder house at 317, may date from the early 19th century. Samuel Peach purchased the lot of 321 and 319 from John Roberts in 1829 for $244. Peach may have enlarged and remodeled, or replaced, an early flounder. In a deed of partition of his estate in 1858, 321 was allotted to John Gibson Peach, who in October 1859 sold it to Joseph Janney for $800. In August 1864 it was conveyed, in trust, to William D. Massey for $1,450. The increases in price suggest the house was further improved over the years.

319. In 1853 A. D. Collinsworth conveyed the lot of 319 to Gilbert S. Minor for $1,500, using the partition wall between a building at the rear of the lot of 319 and the flounder house at 321 to establish the southern boundary of the lot of 319. The three-story brick building on the front of the lot was built by Minor in the spring of 1854. The rear wing of 319 may date from the ownership of Samuel Peach, or earlier. Peach bought the lot in 1829. In January 1855 Minor sold to Lucy S. Thompson for $6,000. On November 1, 1869, Trustees of the Second Presbyterian Church bought it from Lucy's heirs for $4,500. "for a parsonage or residence of the pastor."

317. In 1799 John Fitzgerald became the co-owner, and in 1784 the sole owner, of the quarter block that included the sites of 313 south through 323. When advertised for sale in October 1802, described as a "piece of ground fronting on Wolfe and St. Asaph Streets to be laid off into convenient lots." In 1822 commissioners appointed by the Chancery Court sold, "with the improvements thereon," to John Roberts for $546, that part of the quarter block that included the sites of 317 through 323. It is possible that the "improvements" mentioned were early flounder houses, today 317 and 321. If the house at 317 does incorporate an early flounder house, it has been extensively enlarged and remodeled over the years, as increases in the price indicate. In 1823 Roberts sold to Rachel Painter for $308. In 1845 Rachel and her husband John James conveyed it to Sarah Talbott for $600. In 1848 Sarah sold to William Jamesson for $1,750, and in 1875 Jamesson conveyed to James F. Carlin for $2,750.

307, 305 St. Asaph. Around 1783–1785 Benjamin Shreve and James Lawrason bought and divided the quarter block of which the lots of 307 and 305 are a part. They built adjoining brick houses. Shreve was allotted the southern half and lived at 307. His son and namesake became a sea captain. The Peabody Museum at Salem, Massachusetts, owns a miniature painting of the younger Shreve, and his log of a voyage to Canton, China, in 1819. The senior Shreve died in 1801. In 1815 Edward Stabler purchased 307, and lived there until his death in 1831. In 1854, Richard S. Huck, a son-in-law of Stabler, bought 307. In 1866 it was advertised for sale as a "burnt building" and bought by Samuel F. Gregory. Probably the early house was enlarged and restyled by Huck, or by Gregory. The house at 305 was the home of James Lawrason, father of Thomas Lawrason, who built 301. In May 1810 James' daughter Mercy Ann married Romulus Riggs of Georgetown. Two years later Alice, another daughter, married Elisha Riggs. After James Lawrason died in 1824, in his 71st year, Edward Stabler bought 305. Stabler's son William lived at 305 until his death in 1852. William's sister Rebecca, and his widow, Deborah, lived there until they died, Rebecca in 1866, and Deborah in 1876. In her will Deborah regrets that her books were damaged at "the time my house was burned."

301 St. Asaph. Tax records, and a notice in the *Alexandria Gazette* of December 28, 1816, signed by Charles Norris, establish that this house was built 1815–1816 for Thomas Lawrason, son of James Lawrason. Norris, a workman employed by Lawrason, complains that "sundry ill-disposed persons" have "circulated certain false and malicious reports" about him: that he had charged exorbitant prices for second-hand materials, and had made "improper use" of materials furnished by Lawrason. Norris claims that the charges are false, and that the "reporters thereof" are trying to rob him "of what they think entailed on themselves alone . . . my good name." Lawrason died in 1819. His widow placed her home at the disposal of the Marquis de Lafayette when he was a guest of the town in October 1824.

Also, **601, 603, 605, 607,** brick, 2 stories, gable roof, four units, mid 19th C., renovated; **609,** brick, 2 stories, gable roof, two dormer windows, probably early 19th C.; **610 ½,** clapboard, now aluminum siding, 2 stories with ell, part mansard roof, mid-late 19th C., remodeled 1973; **626, 628, 630,** clapboard, 2 stories, 626 and 628 shed roof, 630 gable roof, triple units, restored; **625,** clapboard, 2 stories, gable roof, dentil cornice, early 19th C., remodeled 1968; **627,** brick, 2 stories, gable roof, modillion cornice, early 19th C.; **631, 633,** flush siding, 2 stories, gable roof, double units, probably mid 19th C., restored; **635, 637,** clapboard, 2 stories, gable roof, areaway, double units, probably early 19th C., remodeled 1968; **639,** clapboard, 2 stories, gable roof, early 19th C.

½ Swift Alley. Probably dates from brick stable built by George Gilpin, who bought the lot in January 1802 from Jonathan Swift for an annual ground rent of $33.33. Gilpin was living in the house now 208 King. In April 1814 Gilpin's heirs sold to Joseph Dean for $400, Dean to assume payment of the ground rent. Now a residence.

2 Swift Alley. Originally a warehouse, probably built by Joseph Riddle around 1795 on a part of a lot he and his partner, James Dall of Baltimore, bought in October 1794. A 1796 insurance policy on adjoining property shows "Joseph Riddle's brick building." An 1803 policy on this warehouse describes it as 40 by 30 feet, three stories high, with a cellar underneath. Now a residence.

Northwest corner with Prince. Captain John Harper's warehouse, built around 1785.

Also, **103** and **105**, brick, 3 stories, old walls incorporated in 19th century buildings; **107**, brick, 3 stories, probably mid 19th C.

215 South, north to Prince. Photograph 1960. Union was laid out around 1780, and soon warehouses lined both sides of the new street. Except for the buildings on the northwest and southwest corners of Union and Prince, the late 18th-early 19th century warehouses have disappeared. Today the mid 19th century warehouses shown in the photograph as 213, 211 and 209, recently have been replaced by town houses. The facades of the mid 19th century buildings at 205 and 203 have been altered.

169

515. Belle Haven Apartments, originally Mount Vernon Cotton Manufactory. Built 1847, four stories, 110 feet long, 50 feet wide. Also then on this quarter block, a "picking house," 40 by 50 feet, an engine house, an office, and a fireproof waste house. In 1854 the factory was employing "upwards of 150 hands, mostly industrious females," the monthly wage twelve to seventeen dollars for an eleven hour day. There were 3,840 spindles for 124 looms, weaving daily nearly 5,000 yards of 36-inch light sheeting. Used to house prisoners of war when Alexandria was occupied by Federal troops 1861–1865. After the war ended, attempts to resume production were unprofitable. Owned by the Robert Portner Brewing Company 1902–1918, and by the Express Spark Plug Company 1918–1928.

428. Under construction when Beal Howard sold to Charles Lee in October 1800. Three months later Charles conveyed to his brother, Edmund Jennings Lee. Of all the Lees who lived in Alexandria, Edmund was the most active in local affairs. Bishop William Meade described him as a "man of great decision and perseverance...obstinate some of us thought... when we disagreed with him." When Lee was mayor, March 1815 to March 1818, he was a "terror to evil doers." The social standing of some Alexandrians who enjoyed gambling did not prevent him from prosecuting them. He was a warden of Christ Church and successfully represented the church in litigation that saved its glebe lands from confiscation. Edmund's son Cassius was an intimate and lifelong friend of Robert E. Lee.

429. Dating from around 1785, restyled around 1850, the earliest Alexandria house associated with the Lees. Built by Philip Richard Fendall, of a prominent Charles County, Maryland, family, often mentioned in Washington's diaries. His second wife, whom he brought from Stratford to his new home in Alexandria, was the widow of Philip Ludwell Lee, and the mother of the "divine Matilda," first wife of Light Horse Harry Lee. While he was serving in Congress, Lee and his wife frequently stopped to visit the Fendalls. Traditionally, it was here that Lee wrote the address delivered by Mayor Dennis Ramsay when Washington passed through Alexandria on his way to assume the presidency. After the death of his second wife, Fendall married, in November 1791, Mary Lee, sister of Light Horse Harry, Charles, Edmund Jennings, and Richard Bland Lee. Fendall died in

1806. His widow lived on in the house with her two children until her death in 1827. Edmund Jennings Lee, Jr., bought the house in 1836 and conveyed it to his father in 1839. The senior Lee died here in 1843. A plat on a 1796 insurance policy shows eight buildings on the quarter block, valued at a total of $11,500, including a "Rabbit House" and a "Pidgeon House." The main dwelling house was valued at $5,000. Admission fee.

407. Photograph shows original rear wing fronting on Princess built around 1798 by Charles Lee. Three-story house fronting on Washington either restyled or replaced. In June 1800 John Adams wrote his wife: "I am particularly pleased with Alexandria. Mr. Lee lives very elegantly, neatly and agreeably there among his sisters and friends and among his fine Lotts of Clover and Timothy. I scarcely know a more eligible situation." Lee attended Princeton. A 1774 newspaper account of the prizes he had won concluded: "This youth, it seems, is but seventeen years of age; and it is thought ... that he will shortly be one of the greatest ornaments of the country." He was appointed Naval Officer of the South Potomac in 1777, Collector of Customs in Alexandria in 1789. He was Attorney General of the United States from December 1795 until 1801. He was counsel for the plaintiffs— Robert T. Hooe and Dennis Ramsay of Alexandria as well as William Marbury of Maryland—in *Marbury v. Madison.* He was one of the attorneys for the defendants Bollman and Swartout, associates of Aaron Burr. After his death in 1815 his house was rented, and from 1817 through 1820 the tenants were the family of Charles' brother, Light Horse Harry, including young Robert E. Lee. In July 1821 Charles' daughter Lucinda, and her husband Walter Jones, conveyed the house to Christ Church in payment of Jones' half-share of the glebe lands. It served for a time as the rectory of the church.

307, 305, 303, 301. Built 1808 by Robert Brockett, "for private families or business." Renovated and restyled around 1852. Owned by Brockett's heirs until 1925. In 1785 Brockett offered his services as a stonecutter or bricklayer, who could "cut, engrave and polish marble for chimney pieces," and "prepare plans and drawings ... agreeable to the taste of any who may please to employ him." He died in 1829.

329. In 1829 John C. Mandell advertised a two-story brick house for rent on this corner. He bought the lot for $400 in 1821. Third story added by Mandell, or by William Gregory, who purchased it at auction in 1832 for $4,000. Gregory came to Alexandria in 1807, when he was eighteen. He owned a dry goods store, selling carpets and woolen goods imported from his family's factory in Kilmarnoch, Scotland. In 1847 he became president of the Alexandria branch of the Farmers' Bank of Virginia, serving until the bank closed in 1866. He died in 1875 in his 87th year. *The History of Old Alexandria, Virginia,* by his daughter, Mary G. Powell, is a valuable source for those interested in the town's early days.

220. Built around 1798 by John Wise. In 1802 Wise's tenant was James Marshall, who was an Assistant Judge of the Circuit Court of the District of Columbia 1801–1803. James' brother John was appointed Chief Justice of the Supreme Court of the United States in 1801, and may have visited here when traveling to and from Washington, D. C. In 1810 Wise sold the house to Jacob Hoffman, who was mayor of Alexandria February 1803–February 1804. In 1825 the widow of James H. Hooe became the owner, and the following spring rented the house to Benjamin Hallowell. Hallowell made interior alterations and established his school here. In 1832 John Lloyd, whose wife was a daughter of Edmund Jennings Lee, bought it at auction.

Family memoirs say that on the Sunday before Lee traveled to Richmond to assume command of the armed forces of Virginia, he attended services at Christ Church and called here, and at the home of Cassius Lee, now 428 North Washington. Dr. Joseph Packard of the Episcopal Seminary, whose wife was a grand-daughter of Charles Lee, was living here when President Lincoln was assassinated. The next morning Federal soldiers called and demanded that crape be put on the front door. That night a large stone was hurled through a front window. The Lloyd family owned the house until 1918. Twice saved from demolition by the Historic Alexandria Foundation. In 1969 purchased by funds contributed by the Hoge Foundation, Federal, State and City governments, and conveyed to the Alexandria Historical Restoration and Preservation Commission. To be used by the Alexandria Library as a repository of books and documents relating to Virginia and Alexandria history.

131. In 1870 Dr. Magnus M. Lewis enlarged and restyled the brick house on the lot when Christopher Neale sold it in 1824. Neale may have lived here when he was mayor of Alexandria from March 1821 to March 1824. Neale also served as Judge of the Orphans' Court, as a director of the Bank of the United States in Washington, D. C., and as president of the Literary Club of Alexandria.

The lot south of 220 North Washington was the site of a brick sugar refinery, shed and warehouse built by Jacob Hoffman. When Benjamin Hallowell was outbid by John Lloyd at the auction of the dwelling house, he bought the sugar refinery buildings and remodeled them for his school. Used as a hospital when Federal troops occupied Alexandria 1861–1865.

109. Washington Street Methodist Church. Until 1849 there was only one Methodist congregation in Alexandria, when some members left and became affiliated with the recently organized Methodist Episcopal Church South. The corner-stone of the original Greek Revival Church was laid in September 1850, and the building was completed in 1851. Present facade 1875. Present interior 1899.

201. Lyceum Hall. Built 1839, restored for Northern Virginia Bicentennial Center 1974, architect Carroll Curtice. Benjamin Hallowell, who headed the group that organized the Lyceum Company in 1838, described it in his *Autobiography*: "a fine building ... with a pediment front supported by four fluted columns, with a triglyph cornice ... surrounded with an iron railing and a beautiful yard of flowers and ornamental shrubbery." The Alexandria Library, established 1794, was in the south room on the first floor, and by 1857 owned around 4,600 books. Lectures were given in the hall on the second floor. Speakers included John Quincy Adams and Caleb Cushing. Debates (political and religious subjects were barred) were held on such questions as: "Is there such a principle in active operation among men as disinterested benevolence?" Civic groups met, and itinerant musicians gave concerts. Used as a hospital 1861–1865. Sold in 1868 to John B. Daingerfield, who converted it into a residence for his daughter and her family. In 1900 conveyed to the wife of Dr. Hugh McGuire. Remained in the McGuire family until 1940, when it was remodeled for office use. In 1970 purchased by the City, with the aid of Federal and State grants, and by private contributions obtained by the Historic Alexandria Foundation, including a donation from the Alexandria Association.

212. Downtown Baptist Church.
Rebuilt 1830, after fire in 1829.
Original church built around 1805,
when the site was conveyed to William Simms and Walker Turner,
Trustees for the Alexandria Baptist
Society. Jeremiah Moore was the
first pastor. In 1954 the First Baptist Church moved to another location. To provide for the continuance of the Baptist ministry in the
downtown area, a group, including
some members of the First Baptist
Church, purchased the building
and established the Downtown
Baptist Church.

220 South to Duke. In 1811 Jonathan Schofield purchased this quarter block from the widow of Henry Piercy, a Revolutionary officer who came to Alexandria from Philadelphia after the Revolution. In 1792 he advertised pottery from his "Earthen Ware Manufactory," a frame building on this quarter block. A substantial amount of Piercy's pottery has been retrieved from a waste pit at the rear of 220. In 1812 Schofield built a row of three two-story and five three-story brick houses (the end house faces on Duke). Only one two-story house still stands, 220, bought by Judge William Cranch in 1817. He lived there until 1821. Cranch was appointed an Assistant Judge of the Circuit Court of the United States for the District of Columbia in 1801, and Chief Judge, in 1806. Described by Charles Francis Adams as "a man of perfectly old-fashioned New England manners," Cranch was a nephew of Abigail Adams, and the great-grandfather of T. S. Eliot, the poet and critic.

John Lloyd bought Schofield's houses at public auction in 1816. The five three-story houses remained in the Lloyd family for many years.

Alexandria Academy. Rear of southeast corner with Wolfe. Now school offices. The minutes of the Trustees of the Academy, owned by Alexandria Washington Masonic Lodge No. 22, give the measurements of the original building, and they are the same as those of the building standing today. The foundation stone was laid September 7, 1785, with Masonic ceremonies. In October 1786 the Virginia Assembly granted a petition to incorporate the Academy, as "Your petitioners have . . . within the last twelve months . . . erected a commodious building fit for an Academy, in which three schools are opened, and about one hundred scholars already admitted." The English School was on the first floor, the Learned Languages School on the second. In 1788 geometry, including practical surveying and navigation, was offered. On the third floor was the Free School, established by General Washington's annual contribution of £50, to educate twenty students whose parents could not pay tuition. Girls were admitted on the understanding that they "give place whenever there . . . be applications for admittance on behalf of Boys." Among the Academy's students before it closed in 1822 were two of Washington's nephews, and Henry and Orlando Fairfax, John Gadsby Chapman, and Robert E. Lee. In January 1823 Samuel A. Marsteller, a grandson of Colonel Philip Marsteller, bought the building and a part of the lot. Tax records show that Marsteller improved the property, perhaps by converting it to residential use.

323, 321. Built by Robert H. Miller on land he bought in 1853. A deed of 1859 conveying 323 to Miller's son Elisha described it as "one of the two brick tenements recently erected by the said Robert H. Miller." Miller owned a large store on King specializing in china and glassware. A man of considerable culture, he served as a Trustee of the Female Orphan Asylum, as president of the Alexandria Water Company, and as the first president of the Citizens' National Bank when it was organized in 1870. In November 1865 Edward S. Hough purchased 321 for $4,500. Photograph 1960. First floor facade now altered.

413, 411, 409, 407, 405, 403, 401.
Houses at 413, 411 may date from
a tenement on the lot when
Thompson Javins bought it from
Christopher Neale in February
1848 for $375. Houses at 409
through 401 built by Charles C.
Smoot after he acquired the land
by several purchases 1846–1847.

417, 415. Built by Thompson Javins
on the vacant lot of ground he
bought in December 1849 for $100.
Photograph 1960. Doorways now
altered.

555. Thomas White bought the half block fronting on the west side of Washington between Wilkes and Gibbon in 1804. Traditionally, the nucleus of the building was "Broomlawn", an early tavern moved from its original site east of Washington street near Hunting Creek. References to "Broomlawn" in early Alexandria newpapers include: (1802) notice of a tea party to be held at "Broomlawn", and its cancellation, the "Broomlawn being priorly engaged;" (1804) notice of a dinner to be held there "with a fine green turtle;" (1809) the public sale of the acre of ground, with improvements, "called Broomlawn;" (1810) notice of a sale by James H. Hooe of Spanish merino sheep at Broomlawn; and (1818) Joseph Tattersall's offer to sell trees and flowering shrubs "at his garden on Broomlawn farm." Building may have been enlarged by Thomas White's son Robert, who in 1843 sold it to his sister for $1,200. Owned by White heirs until 1925, and now the Old Club Restaurant.

606. Roberts Memorial Church.
Built around 1832, restyled. The
Trustees to whom the site was
deeded were Benjamin Waters,
John Shackleford, Benoni Wheat,
Moses O. B. Cawood, Francis Hoy,
James Evans, Philip Hamilton,
Moses Hepburn and Simon Finley.
Church historians say it was estab-
lished as an outgrowth of the First
Methodist Episcopal Church (now
Trinity Methodist.)

Also, **602, 604.** Originally clapboard,
604 now brick veneer, 2 stories, double
units, probably early 19th C., disguised
by recent major alterations.

The "Shadows", or the "Hill House",
an 1854 three-story brick antebellum
dwelling at 617 South Washington,
stood on a large tree-shaded lot until
it was demolished early in 1974.

127, 125. May date from ownership
of James Evans, who bought the
lot in 1809, and in December 1850
conveyed it to Josephine Catherine
Windsor and Martha Frances Armfield Windsor for $2,300.

Also, **110,** flush siding with bricktex, 2
stories, gable roof, adjoining unit
razed, probably mid 19th C.

West Street probably derives its name from its geographical location. When it was laid out, between 1785 and 1798, it was the western boundary of the town.

During the early 1800's, references to West End began to appear in deeds and newspaper notices. A deed of March 12, 1802, conveyed land on the south side of Duke Street extended, "in the addition made by John West to the said town of Alexandria." A deed of November 12, 1803, also conveyed land on the south side of Duke Street extended, "in the suburbs of the Town of Alexandria known by the name of West End." John West conveyed these two parcels of land on October 21, 1796, and on March 27, 1797.

G. M. Hopkins' 1878 map of the Falls Church District of Fairfax County has an inset map of the West End, beginning around Peyton and Duke Streets, extending west on both sides of Duke Street less than half a mile, and ending on Duke Street at a point that would today be parallel with the George Washington National Masonic Memorial.

West End remained in Fairfax County until 1915, when the Supreme Court of Appeals awarded West End, among other parcels of land, to the City of Alexandria.

208, 210. House at 208 may date from a two-story brick dwelling house advertised for rent by George Slacum in 1807. Slacum died in 1810. Building at 210 added by Slacum heirs. When advertised for sale in April 1852, it fronted 42 feet on Wilkes, and contained nine rooms with closets, three pantries, and cellars, in one of which was a dry well, "of great service in summer as a refrigerator." On the lot were a smoke house, carriage house and stables, all of brick. The large garden was filled with flowers, shrubs, and "English walnuts, large Plums, Grapes and Peach trees." Emmeline Thompson, a daughter of George Slacum, bought the property for $3,500 at the 1852 sale. She died before it was conveyed to her. In 1854 it was deeded to her heirs, a son, Samuel P. Thompson, and a daughter, Julia Burke. Julia was the first wife of John Woolfolk Burke, who with Arthur Herbert founded the Burke and Herbert Bank and Trust Company in 1852. Burke handled the sale of Mount Vernon to the Mount Vernon Ladies' Association, and the cash and securities were in his bank when Federal troops occupied Alexandria in 1861. He concealed them in his wife's closet until he was able to smuggle them to the Riggs Bank in Washington, where they remained until after the war. The house, restyled in the Victorian manner, was owned by Burke family until 1945. Restored 1947–1948.

213. In July 1805 John C. Vowell offered for rent a "two-story brick house on Wilkes street, opposite Captain George Slacum's." Probably restyled by A. D. Collinsworth, who bought it in 1852 for $665, and sold it in 1863 for $950.

211, 209. John C. Vowell acquired the site of these two houses from Jacob Cox in 1796. In 1813 Vowell offered to rent a frame tenement on "Wilkes street opposite Mrs. Slacum's." Possibly the house at 211, with the larger frontage, dates from Vowell's ownership. W. J. Lown probably built 209, buying the lot in 1868 for $450, and selling it in 1877 for $1,650.

207, 205. Probably built by Alleghany Smoot, to whom this "lot of ground" was allotted in the 1872 division of the estate of George H. Smoot.

WILKES, WOLFE

South side Wilkes, west of Payne, in St. Paul's cemetery. Grave of the "Female Stranger", who died October 14, 1816, at Gadsby's Hotel. Her gravestone gives her age, 23 years and 8 months, but not her name. The first account of her story is in the *Alexandria Gazette* of December 3, 1836, a reprint of an article in the *Saturday Courier* signed by Lucy Seymour (of Maryland). The writer was told that "a minister of Alexandria had visited her a short time previous to her dissolution, and to him alone, if to any, had she imparted a relation of her career. Her continuance in the city did not exceed a few weeks. A gentleman, who called himself her husband, was her companion, but there were many in Alexandria who suspected the validity of the rites . . . Her early death in a land in which she was a stranger . . . caused considerable excitement in the city; and the subsequent departure of him who called her his wife, suddenly and secretly, tended to increase it."

Tunnel at intersection with Royal. The *Alexandria Gazette* of July 1, 1854, announced: "Workmen are employed on the Railroad Tunnel on Wilkes street at the south end of the City. We hope to see this work speedily completed. It should not be suffered to remain in its present condition any longer." Over a year later, on October 23, 1855, the *Gazette* reported: "Workmen . . . are now finishing the eastern end of the Tunnel."

John Swann's "Stone-Ware Manufactory" was on the north side of Wilkes on a lot he purchased in 1813, beginning 83 feet east of Washington street and continuing east 40 feet, with a depth of half a block. Examples of Swann's pottery have been found on sites of King street buildings demolished in the 1960's.

413 Wilkes. May date from a brick house on Wilkes valued at $3,000, in the list of property in the estate of William Hunter, deceased, 1803. Tax records for 1789 and 1790 list Ludwell Lee as Hunter's tenant on Wilkes. Recently renovated.

Also Wilkes, **427**, clapboard, now bricktex, 2 stories above high basement, 2-story brick ell, gable roof, probably early 19th C., originally, with 429, double units; **429** restored and remodeled with entrance on Pitt.

Also Wilkes, **501, 503, 505**, clapboard, 2 stories, gable roof, triple units, mid 19th C., restored; **507, 509, 511**, clapboard, 2 stories above high basement, triple units, mid 19th C., restored; **527**, clapboard, 2 stories, gable roof, mid 19th C., neglected; **529, 531**, clapboard, 2 stories, gable roof, side leanto, probably mid 19th C., neglected.

Nicholas Cresswell, a young Englishman, arrived in Alexandria on July 11, 1774, with letters of introduction to James Kirk, formerly of Cresswell's parish. Kirk lived on the north side of Wolfe, near the river. Adjoining Kirk was the shipyard of his father-in-law, Thomas Fleming. Fleming served as a town trustee. Kirk was mayor from February 1785 to February 1786. Cresswell found that Kirk and most Alexandrians were "Slebers," his code word for Rebels. His journal tells of the day-by-day developments in northern Virginia 1774–1777.

Southwest corner Wolfe and Union was the site of Daniel Roberdeau's distillery. In 1774, when he was offering it for rent, it was on the Potomac, "below the bank."

Also Wolfe, **106,** originally clapboard, now bricktex, 2 stories, gable roof, early 19th C.

114, 116 Wolfe. Built by Emanuel Francis, who purchased the lot in May 1844 from James Entwisle for $62.50. In March 1854 he conveyed house at 116 to William Fisher for $700.

118, 120 Wolfe. Built by William R. McNeal, to whom James Entwisle sold in May 1844, for $287.50, a lot on the south side of Wolfe extending east from Lee 96 feet 8 inches. The following September McNeal sold the house at 118 to John Bryan for $450.

125, 123 Wolfe. Double units, probably built by George Swain, who in two purchases, in 1845 and 1851, acquired a lot extending from Lee 100 feet east on the north side of Wolfe, for a total of $287. In September 1871 Swain's heirs sold the house at 123 for $350.

221. Joseph Packard sold this corner lot to George H. Smoot in 1839 for $155. In 1844 Smoot conveyed to George W. Maxwell for $258. In 1870 the Chancery Court awarded this "tenement and lot of ground" to Maxwell's widow as her dower.

219. Originally clapboard, now brick veneer. Possibly dates from ownership of Robert Allison, who conveyed it in 1784 for £120. Sold to Mordecai Miller in 1813 for $500. In 1833 partition of Miller's estate, "a tenement and lot of ground."

Also, **206, 208,** brick, 2 stories, replaced frame buildings destroyed in fire of January 1871; **216, 218,** double units with common chimney, brick, 2 stories, gable roof, built by John Wood, Sr., around 1819. 216 and 218 included in photograph of 400 South Fairfax.

215, 213. Site of both houses included in a deed of trust executed by Joseph Cary in November 1796. When advertised in 1802, there was one brick house on the lot, which may be incorporated in 215, or in 213. Present facades may date from the mid-19th century, when owned by the widow of Fielder Luckett, or from the ownership of Joseph Janney. In 1860, Elizabeth, a daughter of Fielder Luckett, and her husband, the Alexandria artist John Gadsby Chapman, then living in Rome, Italy, conveyed Elizabeth's interest in the property to Janney for $125.

211, 209, 207, 205, 203. Houses at 211 and 209 probably built by George Swain, who bought the lot of 211 in April 1839 for $125, and that of 209 in December 1820 for $160. In September 1871 Swain's heirs sold 211· for $510. House at 209 remained in the Swain family until after 1896. Double houses at 207 and 205 built by Laughlin Masterson, who bought the lot in March 1825 for $150. In 1882 house at 207 sold for $350. George Swain built the house at 203, purchasing the site in 1825 for $150. His heirs sold it in 1872 for $850.

212. Built by William Markley, who bought the lot in 1845 for $150, and in 1851 sold to William Wolf, Sr., for $1,200. Renovated after fire in January 1871.

214. This "neat brick dwelling house" was built by William Wolf, Sr., in 1855.

330. Probably built by Robert H. Miller, who was allotted this corner lot in the 1833 partition of the estate of his father, Mordecai Miller. Sold in May 1839 for $700, as a "tenement and lot of ground."

319, 315, 313, 311, 309, 307. Rear flounder house of 319 may date from the ownership of Richard Arell, or from that of his daughter Christiana Hunter. In 1809 Christiana sold to Thomas Preston for $450 the land that included the sites of 319, 315 and 313. In 1847 Philip Rotchford purchased the property for $600. He may have enlarged the house at 319 before he sold it in February 1866, with its present lot boundaries, for $1,000. Houses at 315 and 313 may date from Rotchford's ownership, or from that of Deborah Dyer, to whom Rotchford sold in 1857 for $600 as a "piece of ground . . . with appurtenances." House at 311 built by Johanna Makely, who bought the lot in 1828 for $110, and sold it in 1852 for $1,125. In 1827 Thomas Smith purchased the sites of 309 and 307 for $250. In 1884 he sold 309 for $300, and in 1880, 307 for $800. House at 309 has a false front.

315 Wolfe.

510. Built 1854 by Francis L. Smith on the quarter block his wife Sarah inherited from her father, John C. Vowell. On July 15, 1870, Robert E. Lee wrote his wife from Alexandria: "I have seen Mr. Smith . . . this morning and had with him a long business talk . . . The prospect is not promising." The unpromising prospect was the return of the Arlington estate by the Federal government, on which Smith, Lee's lawyer, was advising him.

415. Nucleus may date from prior to 1788, when tax records show John Butcher as the owner and occupant. A plat of an 1844 survey shows the site of the original house. Butcher was a partner of William Paton in the hardware business, and had an interest in Ezra Kinzey's tanyard. When he died in 1811 his funeral was "from his late dwelling house on Wolfe street."

In 1832 the Female Orphan Asylum and Free School Society of Alexandria purchased the quarter block at the southeast corner of Wolfe and Pitt.

Also, **406**, clapboard, 2 stories, gable roof, false Victorian front, probably late 18th-early 19th C.

710, 712, 714. Double houses at 710 and 712 built by Samuel Beach, who bought the lot for $235 in April 1852. In August 1854 Beach sold the house at 710 for $912. House at 714 may date from ownership of Jonathan Butcher, who bought this quarter block in 1812. In September 1842 Butcher's trustees conveyed the site of 714, and an additional lot on South Columbus, to John Muir for $230. In 1849 Muir sold a "brick tenement" at 714 for $450.

708. A 1930 visitor described this as a "small house, its walls . . . of solid brick covered with weatherboarding, its garden . . . full of crippled old shrubs." Tax records for 1802 show Jonathan Butcher was the occupant, and that the house and quarter block on which it stands were valued at $1,000.

716, 718. Built by Jonathan Butcher after 1812. In 1847 Butcher's trustees sold these "two tenements" for $440.

827. The proportions and style of this building suggest an inn or public house, but when it was advertised for sale in 1874 it was as a "three-story brick tenement." The original site, bought by Jacob Muddiman in 1863, was a lot fronting 16 feet on Alfred, and 73 feet on Wolfe.

Also, **800**, brick, 2 stories, stuccoed, gable roof, probably early 19th C.; **801, 803, 805,** brick, 2 stories above basement, triple units, gable roof, elaborate molded cornice, built by S. E. Tucker 1855.

INDEX

INDEX

INDEX

INDEX

INDEX

INDEX

INDEX

Additional copies of
this book may be purchased
through your favorite
bookshop or ordered directly
from

EPM Publications, Inc.
Box 490
McLean, Virginia 22101
Phone: (703) 442-7810

The price per copy is $14.95
including postage and handling.
Virginia residents, please add
58¢ tax per copy.